PATRICK & BE~
MOU~
MILWAUK~

Praise for . . .

Transformation Thinking:

"FILLED WITH EXAMPLES OF THE MAGIC THAT OCCURS
when people and organizations overcome the fear of change. They can go beyond
even their expectations to do the undoable. Don't just read it, just do it!"
— J. Kermit Campbell, President and CEO, Herman Miller, Inc.

"PROVIDES AN EXCELLENT GUIDE
to improving individual and group thinking skills."
— Daniel Burrus, leading technology forecaster and author of *Technotrends*

"IT IS BECOMING INCREASINGLY IMPERATIVE
that any 'leading' organization must indeed become a 'learning organization.'
Transformation Thinking provides the vehicle to make that journey . . . A valuable
resource that translates theory to pragmatic, real-world examples."
— Edward E. Scannell, CMP, CSP, trainer and author of *Games Trainers Play*

"A 'MUST-HAVE' FOR MANAGERS,
teachers, trainers, consultants, and anyone who wants to grow creatively . . .
Every page contains something new and thought-provoking."
— Arthur VanGundy, Ph.D., Professor of Communications, University of Oklahoma

"OUTLINES MANY TOOLS AND TECHNIQUES
to help managers develop the transformational thinking required
for survival in the 21st century."
— Weston H. Agor, Ph.D., Professor, University of Texas at El Paso,
founder, The Global Intuition Network

"IF YOU WORK WITH GROUPS, STUDY THIS BOOK!
Teamwork fails most often because members can't/won't/don't communicate.
This book provides 'conceptual pry-bars' to open up even the most
stuck groups. This.stuff works!"
— Woodrow Sears, Ph.D., consultant

continued on next page . . .

PATRICK & BEATRICE HAGGERTY LIBRARY
MOUNT MARY COLLEGE
MILWAUKEE 2, WISCONSIN 53222

"OUR STATE GOVERNMENT QUALITY INITIATIVE,
Texas Quality Service, creates opportunity for employees to use their brains on the job
— individually and collectively. This book shows them how!"
— Ann Richards, former Governor of Texas

"WINDS UP THE DNA CLOCK FOR METAMORPHOSIS
TO A NEW PLANE OF POTENTIAL
for individuals and organizations."
— Michael Munn, Ph.D., Director of Creativity,
Lockheed Missiles & Space Company

"This is a book for people who are either running companies or managing
departments and waiting for someone in their company to be innovative.
STOP WAITING AND BEGIN READING."
— Jack Stack, CEO, Springfield ReManufacturing Corp.

"SHOWS ALL PEOPLE HOW TO BECOME ONE OF THOSE FEW
WHO ARE MAKING A REAL CONTRIBUTION TO
THE WORLD AROUND THEM."
— Jim Cathcart, Author of *Relationship Selling* and *The Acorn Principle*

"THIS IS A WEAR-OUT-THE-PAGES BOOK . . .
A MUST READ, STUDY AND USE BOOK!
The message is about the improved bottom line for today and tomorrow
in a continually changing world."
— Ray Payn, Multi-media Software Developer

"Once I finished reading this book, it settled into my memory like a cat curling
up by the stove. It will be there for a long time . . .
READERS WILL FIND IT IRRESISTIBLE."
— Michael Michalko, Author of *Thinkertoys*

"SUCH LUCID WRITING ABOUT AN ELUSIVE SUBJECT!
And the illustrative anecdotes are alive, vibrant and convincing. I look forward to
introducing *Transformation Thinking* to my workshop participants."
— Anne Robinson, Creativity, Communication & Common Sense

"IT'S A BOOK YOU DON'T WANT TO PUT DOWN."
— Barbara Gaughen, President, Gaughen Public Relations

"ANOTHER MARVELOUS CONTRIBUTION TO CORPORATE AMERICA.
I love your research, references, stories, and the easy way you
make the difficult doable."
— Marsh Fisher, CEO, IdeaFisher Systems, Inc.

"GIVES YOU THE BASIS FOR MAKING SWEEPING CHANGE
IN YOUR ORGANIZATION.
At West Paces, we started working together in teams and thinking
visually five years ago . . . the results exceed all of our expectations."
— Chip Caldwell, Vice-President, Juran Institute,
former CEO of West Paces Ferry Hospital

"Here's a major key to success and failure in today's rapidly changing world:
Get smart or go broke. Success in the information age is determined by brain power.
ANY ORGANIZATION OR PERSON THAT WANTS TO BOOST THEIR
LEARNING AND CREATIVE THINKING SKILLS
NEEDS TO READ *TRANSFORMATION THINKING*."
— Michael LeBoeuf, Ph.D., Author of *Fast Forward* and
How to Win Customers and Keep Them for Life

"THIS BOOK IS ENJOYABLE AND UNDERSTANDABLE.
But most important it provides the reader with an excellent approach to
improving an organization's performance
in the vital area of creative or innovative thinking."
— Dar Richardson, Materials Manager, Enviro Tech Pumpsystems

"THIS BOOK IS FULL OF POWER AND PUNCH . . .
PACKED FULL OF OVERARCHING TRUTHS AND
GROUNDED IN PRACTICAL APPLICATION."
— Melody Starling, teacher

"GREAT WORK."
— Vic Sassone, Consultant, Total Quality Management

"Smart companies need smart people.
TRANSFORMATION THINKING SHOWS YOU
HOW EASY IT IS TO GIVE EVERYONE IN YOUR ORGANIZATION
A BRAIN BOOST!"
— Tamara Lufkin, Marketing Manager, Microsoft

"OFFERS ALL-WHEEL DRIVE SOLUTIONS TO THE
RUT-FILLED BUSINESS ROAD."
— Bruce Hanna, President, Enterprise Development

"A BULL'S-EYE ON A MOVING TARGET!
Transformation Thinking requires leading the mark. This book delivers
a rare balance of seasoned counsel and calibrated strategies."
— Larry L. Axline, practitioner and author, Human Resources
and Organizational Development

"GREAT MATERIAL, TIMELY MESSAGE."
— Karen Bentley, teacher

"AN EXCITING PROJECT AND DEFINITELY VERY
ENJOYABLE READING."
— Richard C. Emanuel, Ph.D., professor

"THIS BOOK HAS THE POTENTIAL TO MAKE A DIFFERENCE.
I truly appreciate the concreteness and lack of jargon."
— Lee Powell, teacher

Mindmapping:

"A NO-NONSENSE, PRACTICAL, EXTREMELY READABLE GUIDE
to help you put your creative powers to work!"
— Michael LeBoeuf, bestselling author of *Fast Forward* and *How to
Win Customers and Keep Them for Life*

"AN EXCELLENT AND WORTHY ACCOMPLISHMENT."
— Tony Buzan, author of *Use Both Sides of Your Brain*

Berkley Books by Joyce Wycoff

MINDMAPPING

TRANSFORMATION THINKING (WITH TIM RICHARDSON)

Most Berkley Books are available at special quantity discounts for bulk purchases for sales promotions, premiums, fund raising, or educational use. Special books or book excerpts can also be created to fit specific needs.

For details, write or telephone Special Markets, The Berkley Publishing Group, 200 Madison Avenue, New York, New York 10016; (212) 951-8891.

PATRICK & BEATRICE HAGGERTY LIBRARY
MOUNT MARY COLLEGE
MILWAUKEE, WISCONSIN 53222

Transformation Thinking

Tools and Techniques That Open the Door to Powerful New Thinking for Every Member of Your Organization

JOYCE WYCOFF

with TIM RICHARDSON
FOREWORD BY GEORGE LAND

B
BERKLEY BOOKS, NEW YORK

TRANSFORMATION THINKING

A Berkley Book / published by arrangement with the author

PRINTING HISTORY
Berkley trade paperback edition / May 1995

All rights reserved.
Copyright © 1995 by Joyce Wycoff.
This book may not be reproduced in whole or in part,
by mimeograph or any other means, without permission.
For information address: The Berkley Publishing Group,
200 Madison Avenue, New York, New York 10016.

ISBN: 0-425-14374-0

BERKLEY®
Berkley Books are published by The Berkley Publishing Group,
200 Madison Avenue, New York, New York 10016.
BERKLEY and the "B" design
are trademarks belonging to Berkley Publishing Corporation.

PRINTED IN THE UNITED STATES OF AMERICA

10 9 8 7 6 5 4 3 2 1

658.4
W977t
1995

SPECIAL THANKS

This book stands on ground broken by Alex Osborn, Sydney J. Parnes, E. Paul Torrance, W.J.J. Gordon, George Prince, Edward deBono, Silvano Arieti, J.P. Guilford, Arthur VanGundy, Tony Buzan, Peter Russell and countless others who have explored the world of the mind and captured many of its secrets.

We were fortunate to have so many people contribute generously of their time to share experiences, ideas and philosophies. Thanks to all of you for making this book possible!

We are deeply grateful to:
Vicki Davis, who started the ball rolling while she was coaching the quality program for West Paces Ferry Hospital;
Chip Caldwell, CEO with West Paces who "walks the talk" as well as any CEO around;
Jack Stack, Springfield ReManufacturing, a CEO who led an incredible transformation and showed us what an organization could be;
Charlie Soap, Ron Gonzales, and Bertha Alsnay with the Cherry Tree Project who showed us another dimension of transformation;
George Land, a generous and wise leader;
Ray Payn who helped us see the patterns;
Nancy Margulies for her wonderful illustrations and chapter on mindmapping and mindscaping; and
Harriet Eckstein and Lillian Payn for taking our visual doodles and turning them into graphic communication.

Special thanks to:
Steve Grovender and Patti Konsti with 3M;
Chuck Nakell with Inspiration Software;
Marsh Fisher, founding guru of IdeaFisher;
Marlee Parker with Chandler Parker Public Relations;
Harvey Greenberg with Polaroid Corporation;
Sue Calhoun & Chris Allshouse and the staff of University Medical Center Media Center;
Linda Honold with Leadership Dynamics;
Pat Sullivan of Sullivan & Associates;
Michael Tattersoll with Scientific Generics;
Lee Powell, Melody Starling, Karen Bentley and Hilton Smith with the Foxfire Organization;

Doug Hall at Eureka! Mansion:
Beth Jarman and Ron Bell at Leadership 2000;
Renee Rogers at Intermedics Orthopedics;
Ed Preston with Ed Preston & Associates;
Dar Richardson with EnviroTech;
Thomas Stewart with *Fortune* magazine;
Patricia Mettrick with Mine Safety Appliance;
Mark Morgan with Grumman Technical Services;
Dave Gunby with EDS;
Margaret Wheatley, E.D., University of Utah;
Susan Ashford, Ph.D., University of Michigan;
Arthur VanGundy, Ph.D., University of Oklahoma;
Michael W. Munn, Ph.D., Lockheed Missiles & Space Co.;
Jerry McNellis, The McNellis Group;
Margaret Downey with CSX Transportation;
Craig Ellerbroek, Martin Marietta Information Systems;
Jim Shenk with CEC Instruments;
Clayton Lee, inventor of Orbiter treadmill;
Bob Martin, International Business Resources, Inc.;
Fred Altomare with IBM;
Kevin Krueger with Manco, Inc.;
Russell Thompson with Branch Banking & Trust;
Richard Hadden, consultant;
Megan Montgomery at Patagonia;
Greg Diehl with Granite Rock;
Natalie Yount at Microsoft Corporation;
Adrianna Foss, Karen Madden and Paul Orfalea with Kinko's;
Ellen Placey with Old St. Patrick's Church;
Ken Zion and Jim Caldwell with Domino's Pizza;
Joan Helms with Florida Prevention Association.

The following consultants shared wisdom, ideas and valuable guidance:
Woody Sears, Vic Sassone, Anthony Nagle, Ray Payn, Jim Cathcart,
and Dolores Forsythe.

**And special thanks to the following people who read the rough drafts and
offered ideas and support:**
Tom McDaniel, Tamara Lufkin, Paul Golus, Anne Robinson, Dean Radetsky, Barbara
Gaughen, Chuck Nakell, Karen Bentley, Medody Starling, Dameron Williams, Woody
Sears, Vic Sassone, Anthony Nagle, Jim Seroka, Ph.D., Bill Stubbs, Rich Emmanuel,
Ph.D., Marshall Case, John McNally, Nancy Margulies, Bruce Hanna, Jim Carpenter,
Jerry Wetzel, Barbara Cox, Jane Gladue, Don and Lois Richardson, and Jane Ellis.

Your help and support made this a much better book!

DEDICATION

This book is dedicated to you, the reader,
the holder of the vital spark of potential.
May something you find here help you grow
and may you find a way to pass it on.

Also to our best friends, cheerleaders and spouses:
Richard and Adele

FOUR TRANSFORMATION THINKING PRINCIPLES

❖ **We *all* need transformation.**

The four dark horsemen (war, famine, pestilence and death) still stalk our world, sapping its vitality and leaving us depleted, hungry, sick and fearful.

❖ **Transformation depends on better thinking.**

Refining our vision, setting goals, developing and implementing plans, and evaluating results is a continuing process of shedding old skin in order to make new . . . a process of transformation that requires a better way of thinking.

❖ **Everyone *can* think better.**

A mind is a terrible thing to waste. The awful truth is that we're wasting millions of them. Literally no one uses the mind's full potential.

❖ **The tools for better thinking are available.**

Many of the tools included here have been used for decades by academics and professionals. They are presented here in a way that allows them to be used by anyone in any organization.

Suggestion:

This book is your personal guide to transformation — a road map to the skills needed to achieve your goals.

So, please keep a notebook handy to record your ideas and answers to the questions scattered throughout the book.

Enjoy . . . and transform!

CONTENTS

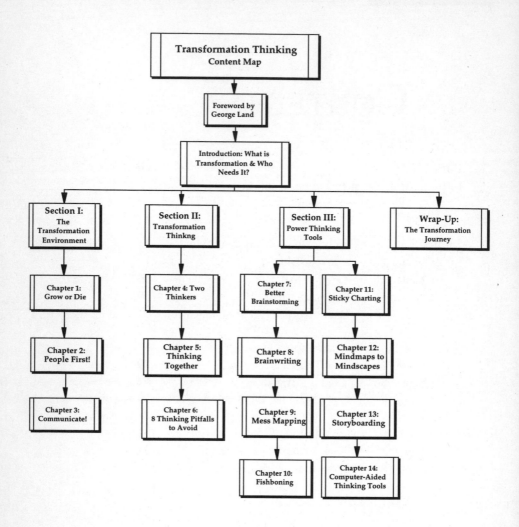

Transformation Thinking
Content Map

Foreword by
George Land

Introduction: What is
Transformation & Who
Needs It?

Section I:
The
Transformation
Environment

Section II:
Transformation
Thinkng

Section III:
Power Thinking
Tools

Wrap-Up:
The Transformation
Journey

Chapter 1:
Grow or Die

Chapter 4: Two
Thinkers

Chapter 7:
Better
Brainstorming

Chapter 11:
Sticky Charting

Chapter 2:
People First!

Chapter 5:
Thinking
Together

Chapter 8:
Brainwriting

Chapter 12:
Mindmaps to
Mindscapes

Chapter 3:
Communicate!

Chapter 6:
8 Thinking Pitfalls
to Avoid

Chapter 9:
Mess Mapping

Chapter 13:
Storyboarding

Chapter 10:
Fishboning

Chapter 14:
Computer-Aided
Thinking Tools

FOREWORD

Leaders in the world's business community have long realized that their success depends on creatively working in a rapidly changing environment. However, in the midst of massive quality, creative and other training programs introduced over the past few decades, determining which path to follow has been a difficult and elusive decision for many executives. Many companies have tried them all, from TQM on down, experimenting with their employees to see what would work. Unfortunately, many of the programs introduced on a wide scale have been driven by the very structure that needs changing: the organizational hierarchy. When change is mandated from the leaders of the company, and when that leadership is largely inaccessible to employees, movement in a new direction is highly unlikely. As we have been telling clients for years, organizations don't change, people do. But people don't change by proxy or on demand; they must be enrolled in the new vision, and their participation must come organically and willingly for real transformation to take place.

Transformation! There's that word again. It has become a modern buzzword in the corporate community. One of the advantages of buzzwords, of course, is that everyone begins to speak the same language, and supposedly begins to move in the same direction — forward. However, by throwing such a word around on a regular basis, a word originally intended to imply such vast change that it feels like a death and complete new beginning, dilutes its meaning and its impact. When we speak of transformation, we are referring to a change of direction on all levels within the organization, a change not only of how we work, but how we think, interact, participate and perform. Transformation of an organization is a process upon which everyone must willingly embark, knowing that it is a journey requiring commitment, intention and full participation.

❖ Transformation: Death and a new beginning

Joyce Wycoff and Tim Richardson demonstrate their deep respect and understanding of the process of transformation in *Transformation Thinking*. Their extensive research into companies that have led the way into the murky waters of transformation reveals that the process is not only possible but tremendously rewarding. And the rewards don't simply reflect the bottom line of the spreadsheet, but the quality of work, the excitement of employees, as well as a general sense people begin to have that they are not simply doing a job, but that their job has meaning. In transformational organizations people know they are adding value not only to their organization, but to the community as well.

Wycoff and Richardson touch on the very important concept that in order to step out onto the limb of change, everyone must have a larger picture of the whole. Part of this is established with the creation of a compelling vision that inspires every member of an organization, from the factory floor to the executive board. On an even larger and more inclusive scale, however, is the idea that everyone in the organization is a vital and creative part of the whole, that they are being pulled by their commitment to the vision to a powerful and dynamic future, and that everyone is connected in this giant tapestry called life. As people begin to feel included in the future of the companies for which they work, this feeling begins to extend into the larger community, and the connection to the world outside one's immediate environment becomes more real and tangible. It seems a natural extension to give to the community when companies are rewarded by that community for doing work that offers meaning to the lives of individual employees.

This world view is a sharp contrast to the competitive, win-lose environments we have been long taught to accept. We have named this expansive outlook the Creative Worldview, implying the three cornerstone concepts of creativity, connection and future pull, or a vision centered environment. Leaders who deeply recognize the creative potential of their employees, who commit fully to a vision of the future rather than to the fears from the past, and who also feel a larger responsibility to their communities stand out as the pioneers of creating transformational organizations.

Transformational Thinking is an exciting book because it offers tremendous insights into how leaders, facilitators and employees at all levels of today's organizations can integrate the Creative Worldview into decision making, product development, idea generation, and many other daily activities in corporate life. Their approach offers the tangible techniques necessary to bring members of an organization together behind a common vision, proven methods for connecting people within the company, as well as bridging the gap that too often exists between businesses and their communities. The other cornerstone of the Creative Worldview, creativity, is specifically addressed in most of their processes. It is imperative, in this era of expanding information and technology that people not only be productive, but that they know how to ask questions and generate the ideas that will lead them into a successful future. Growth and development can only be achieved if everyone is involved and entrusted to make creative decision. These authors have gone to great lengths to offer many new methods and techniques that bring forth the creativity of everyone involved. Equally importantly, they have explored at some depth the role management must be willing to play in encouraging people to grow and explore new possibilities in themselves.

In a sense, *Transformation Thinking* is creative thinking from a much broader base. It is born of a larger, more connected perspective, is inclusive and demands participation. Thinking of this kind breaks down long standing barriers, opens new vistas and greatly stimulates peak performance. When people are enrolled in the direction an organization is moving, and feel that their input is not only requested but honored and implemented, enthusiasm and performance can only increase. A working environment of this kind stimulates continuous breakthrough thinking, product improvement and growth, both of the organization and the individuals within it.

The concepts presented in Joyce Wycoff and Tim Richardson's book are not only beneficial to today's business community, they are part of the foundation we must build on our way to a more creative, dynamic future. The stories presented of organizations and leaders who have already made the leap from our traditional business perspectives into a Creative Worldview, where people are honored as tremendous resources and management is in service to the larger vision, paint a portrait of what is possible if we begin to think transformationally. I highly recommend this book to people working at all levels of organizations who not only want to prepare for a vastly different future, but who wish to be at the forefront of creating it.

— George Land, co-author of *Breakpoint and Beyond* and CEO of Leadership 2000

Transformation Thinking

WHAT IS TRANSFORMATION AND WHO NEEDS IT?

Never doubt that a small group of thoughtful,
committed citizens can change the world —
indeed, it's the only thing that ever has.
— Margaret Mead

It's easy to look around us and see degeneration and chaos. Schools that don't educate . . . governmental gridlock . . . gangs and neighborhood violence . . . pregnant teenagers . . . drug and alcohol abuse . . . massive unemployment . . . homelessness . . . despair. And yet, if we look closely we can see glimmers of hope in every sea of darkness. In Oklahoma, one community project reduced crime by 90%; in the North Georgia mountains, students who initially saw no purpose to learning English later produced a series of best-selling books; and in Springfield, Missouri, a technically bankrupt company became a source of wealth for its employee-owners.

The question is "Why?" Why do some schools work miracles while others remain a battleground between teachers, students, parents and administrators? Why do some community projects make enormous progress while others stay mired in apathy and failure? Some churches thrive and grow while others wither, some businesses prosper by generating new ideas, products and services while others struggle and lay-off thousands of workers who never thought it could happen to them. *Why?*

The Question and the Search

We're living in a difficult time of rapid change, global competition, and failing institutions. But some organizations make it while others fail. *Why?* Is there a common thread running through the organizations that flourish, differentiating them from the ones that run aground?

That critical question prompted our search. We have spent the past several years studying and talking to people to discover the answers. We interviewed business people, educators, government officials, community development workers, philosophers and consultants. While our prime interest was business, we followed stories of unusual success in many different fields trying to find clues. And, we did indeed find answers . . . in very unexpected places . . . places like Cherry Tree, Oklahoma, and a nation-wide teacher development project with its roots in rural Georgia (See Section II). We found answers in an old church in Chicago (See Section III), in several new generation computer software programs (See Chapter 14), in dozens of ground-breaking companies (stories scattered throughout the text) and in one 20-year-old biology book (See Chapter 1).

The Answer

As we talked to people in different businesses, organizations and professions across the country, we kept finding pieces of the puzzle of why some organizations are wildly successful while others flounder. One of the biggest pieces came from Herman Miller, Inc., an extraordinary company that was practicing participative management long before it became a buzzword. Herman Miller's 1992 annual report is the size of a paperback book with the first 80 pages devoted to snippets of philosophy from the new CEO, J. Kermit Campbell.

Included in the report are statements on singing, laughter, viticulture, and Herman Miller's picnics as well as the somewhat more expected management philosophy statements on delighting customers, continuous improvement, the role of a manager, and participation and teamwork. In this amazing statement of philosophies and finances, Campbell refers to a book by George Ainsworth Land, titled *Grow or Die*. That reference led us to the twenty-year-old biology-oriented philosophy book where we found an answer that blasted open our thinking.

2

Before you get too excited, however, please remember that answers are often easy; implementation is the hard part. Both of us are committed to results so we knew it wasn't enough to share answers, we needed to provide specific ideas that could be implemented in a wide variety of organizations. These ideas can be used to help organizations identify and achieve their vision ... which is what we call transformation. Any organization that doesn't yet know quite where it wants to go or hasn't discovered the formula for getting there is a candidate for transformation.

In case you are one of the fortunate few who doesn't feel the need for transformation today, keep in mind that it's highly likely that you will need it tomorrow, next month or next year. Change isn't going to stop any time soon. A recent *Wall Street Journal* article estimates that the "reengineering" of organizations could cause a loss of *25 million jobs!* The very nature of change guarantees that at some point you will need to completely rethink your organization and move in a new direction. When this is done successfully, it is transformation and it looks like magic: remarkable changes happen that you would never have thought possible.

One of the answers we discovered was that an organization can't transform itself until it transforms its thinking. And, thinking within an organization is defined as the mental activity of every member of the organization . . . all the idea generation, learning and skill development, exchange of information, development of strategic directions, project planning, communication, market research, problem solving, process improvement and quantum leaps that make up the total intellectual activity of the organization.

Transformation thinking is a powerful bottom-line technique but it's not just about business. It is a basic set of skills we need in our schools, government, communities and in our families. When these skills are shared and used by a group of people to achieve a common objective, incredible things happens. One of our favorite examples comes from Cherry Tree, Oklahoma.

Cherry Tree's Field of Dreams

State Highway 59 winds south out of Stilwell through the gentle Oklahoma hills. This is heartland America: a person-to-

❖
Answers are easy. Implementation comes harder.

❖
Transformation defined

❖
Will you survive "reengineering?"

❖
Transformation begins with a change in thinking.

3

person place not much concerned with high tech problems and international feuds. The two-lane blacktop cuts through farm fields and pastures fringed with buck brush and scrub oak woods.

However, the serene, muted beauty of the countryside belies the troubled history of Cherry Tree, a community just off the almost-deserted highway. It is familiar territory — a poor, rural community plagued by drugs and alcohol, crime and a sense of defeat. Kids with nothing to do; adults with no hope . . . more a cluster of misery than a community. But, Cherry Tree had something special ... and it did something remarkable.

Most of Cherry Tree's 300 residents are members of the Cherokee Nation, and by 1990, The Nation had participated in several uniquely successful community development programs under the leadership of Chief Wilma Mankiller. Hearing of those successful programs, the Cherry Tree parents who were tired of losing their kids to drugs, crime and alcohol thought there might be a way to solve their problems. They approached Chief Mankiller for help but her schedule was already over-booked so she volunteered her husband, Charlie Soap, Director of the Christian Children's Fund for the Oklahoma area.

"I remember the first time we met in 1990," recalls Soap. "The parents came and asked me to help them do some youth projects. They didn't know what to do or how to get started." Charlie Soap's life is deeply etched in his strong, dark face. His voice and eyes are gentle and protective as he speaks with passion about the Cherry Tree Project.

With that first group of parents was Ron Gonzales, father of three boys. For years Gonzales had gazed across the pastures and scrub oak but instead of seeing the northeastern Oklahoma hills, he saw a baseball diamond and players in white uniforms standing on an emerald green field. He heard shouts and cheers of families and friends. He saw a community of people playing together. But, the vision had always faded into the reality of trees and weeds.

When Soap asked the parents what they wanted, Gonzales immediately replied: *A ball field.* "I was amazed," stated Soap. "They had all these problems — vandalism, drugs, school drop-out . . . an amazingly high suicide rate. And they wanted a ball field. So I asked why."

Gonzales had an explanation, "The kids don't like each other. They're fighting all the time and always getting in trouble. If we could form a baseball team or several teams throughout the community, they would become teammates. They'd support each other and become friends. They wouldn't be fighting; they'd be playing ball together."

The underlying principle of the community development process used by Soap is that everything comes from the community. If they wanted a ball field, it was his job to help them organize and build a ball field. The group formed a Youth Council and began to hold fund raisers. The kids were excited about the possibility of playing ball and they started pushing their parents to help even more. A temporary site was found and work started with some of the kids working from early morning till late at night.

But, change doesn't come easily. Several young bullies delighted in tearing up the field as fast as Gonzales and his Youth Council built it. Gonzales is a quiet, patient man and he kept the kids calm. He would say, "Don't get mad. Don't retaliate. Let's just fix it back up and then ask them to come play." But the bullies refused to join them and continued to vandalize the ball field.

The turning point came when the Youth Council was offered tickets to a Texas Rangers game. No one in Cherry Tree had ever been to a professional baseball game. The kids were all crazy to go, but they looked at their bigger goals and decided to share some of their precious tickets with the bullies . . . who accepted this offer. The trip made the bullies part of the group and they became champions and protectors of the project.

After that trip, momentum started gathering and more and more people wanted to be involved. In the group meetings, people began to think bigger. They wanted something more than just one temporary ball field. They wanted a permanent place where everyone could play . . . from the little kids to the adults. Someone remembered a plot of land owned by the Cherokee Nation currently being used for cattle grazing but big enough for a recreation area for the entire community. They approached the tribal council with a proposal and suddenly Cherry Tree had 115 acres to develop. Gonzales' vision flickered back to life.

Of course, it's one thing to design something on paper and quite another to make it happen. Without tractors, bulldozers

5

or a building loan, Cherry Tree's field of dreams didn't look very promising. However, almost everyone in the community showed up with their garden rototillers, hoes, shovels, spades and rakes. Painfully, rock by rock and root by root, they carved a ball field out of a cow pasture.

Today, if you take State Highway 59 south from Stilwell and turn right at the Cherry Tree Head Start center, you can follow a dirt road through the woods till it opens up to a broad expanse ringed by oak trees. If you're lucky, Gonzales will come down from the brand new community tractor and you can sit on the bleachers facing the first ball field and listen to him describe the rest of the Cherry Tree Project: three additional ball fields, a t-ball field, a walking/jogging path through the woods, a bicycle motocross designed and built by the little kids, a gymnasium, a wellness program, and a Cherry Tree Project store.

❖
10:1 reduction
in crime

And the bottom line? Local law enforcement officials report that before the ball field project, 50 percent of all the calls they received were from or about Cherry Tree. Today they generate only 5 percent of the total calls. Each member of the community "owns" the Cherry Tree Project and there is a lot of pride in what they have accomplished and what they intend to accomplish. Cherry Tree has become a community with a future . . . a field of dreams with very real results.

The basic rules of the community development process used by Cherry Tree has applications for all organizations:

❏ Definition of the problem and all potential solutions have to come from the people.

❏ Participation has to be voluntary.

❏ Find a way to involve the holdouts.

The Transformation Process

This book is about the thinking it takes to create transformation like Cherry Tree's . . . transformation that often looks like magic. It has two fundamental beliefs:

❏ people can learn to develop their thinking skills and improve the quality of their ideas.

❏ organizations that encourage and develop thinking skills in every member of the organization, create an environment where transformation and success flourish.

The transformation process that we will be describing in the coming chapters looks like the following:

Today's Organization

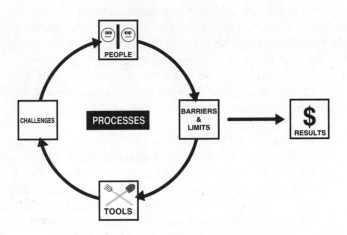

Thinking Tomorrow's Organization

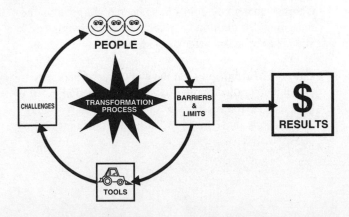

Notice that the process doesn't prevent problems and challenges nor does it eliminate barriers and limitations. However, by creating a different environment for people to work together and by giving them powerful thinking tools and processes, the barriers and limitations are overcome to create greater results.

The magic of transformation can't be guaranteed but it can be encouraged and it only comes from one source . . . people. People working together, thinking together, laughing together, and people striving together for a common goal. While magic sometimes happens in one mind alone, it most often occurs as sparks fly between minds.

Transformation Thinking can help you catch the sparks. In the following chapters, you will find tools and techniques for implementing transformation in your organization . . . whether it's a business, school, church, or government agency.

To help you learn and remember the ideas presented, we have included the following format helpers:

❑ **Coming Attractions Windows** — the first page of each chapter shows a window highlighting the main chapter ideas. The window icons are repeated at the edge of each page. This graphic representation of the material will help you remember ideas and will also help you quickly find material that you would like to review.

❑ **Frameworks & Models** — throughout the book, theories and principles have been reduced to visual models that will help you thoroughly understand the material.

❑ **Gems** — many key points have been highlighted in the margin with a diamond marker. The wide margins give you space to make notes or mark your own key ideas.

❑ **Chapter Mindmaps** — at the end of each chapter is a visual map (called a mindmap and explained in detail in Chapter 12) of the main ideas in the chapter. You may want to copy those maps and add your own notes, ideas and associations.

❏ **Ponder Breaks** — Throughout the more theoretical first two sections, you will find Ponder Breaks which give you a chance to stop and think about the material and apply it to your particular situation.

There are two sayings which are used frequently in the adult education world. The first is: *Tell 'em what you're going to tell 'em; . . . tell 'em; . . . and tell 'em what you told 'em.*

The Coming Attractions Windows provide a graphic outline of the chapter and visual icons to prompt your memory. It tells the reader what you're going to tell them. The gems, frameworks, models and the chapter mindmaps then reinforce the message and improve memory retention by "telling them what you told them."

The second bit of wisdom is an old Chinese proverb:
I hear and I forget.
I see and I remember.
I do and I understand.

Ideas presented only in a verbal context are quickly forgotten. When pictures are combined with the text, the ideas are remembered more easily. However, it is only when someone actively works with ideas and applies them to real situations that they are truly understood and incorporated. The Ponder Breaks are designed to help you make use of the material in Sections I and II. They give you a chance to stop and think about the material in connection to your specific situations.

The tools and techniques covered in Section III are presented in detail to help you use them in your organization. We would like to encourage you to try them and reap the benefits that come when you turn every member of your organization into a power thinker!

THE
TRANSFORMATION
ENVIRONMENT

Epiphany: a sudden perception of the essential
nature or meaning of something;
an intuitive grasp of reality
through something usually simple and striking.

We tend to think of epiphany as being a mystical or religious moment ... and it is — even when it isn't related to the mystical or the religious.

We'd like to share an epiphany we experienced as we were working on this book. But, before we get to our particular blinding moment of truth, we'd like to take you back in time . . . far back. Back to the days of Jurassic — before it was a park. Assume that you live one cave over from the Flintstones and on a sunny Saturday you decide that it's time to throw some dinosaur steaks on the grill. You call all the designated hunters together and head off to the dinosaur stomping grounds with your clubs on your shoulders.

After a few hours you reach the edge of a cliff and forty feet down you see a juicy-looking brontosaurus. Your buddy Goober holds up his club and says, "I'll get 'em." Before you can say anything, Goober jumps and lands splat where the dinosaur was. You scratch your head, feel your tiny, unevolved brain churning, and wonder what went wrong. Several possibilities come to mind:

a. The dinosaur stomped on Goober while making
   his get-away.
b. Goober jumped wrong.
c. Cliff jumping is unhealthy for cave folk.

11

I

Because you don't understand the laws of nature . . .
especially the law of gravity . . . you don't know what to do next.
Maybe if you just jump a different way, you could safely hop
down and follow the dinosaur? Or should you just look for a
different dinner? How many hunters will become cliff fodder
before it's apparent that leaping off cliffs is not the thing to do?

The quandary of these cave folk may seem elementary
but it is directly related to our epiphany . . . and we guarantee it
has nothing to do with dinosaur steaks.

Fads, Theories, and Quick Fixes

Over the past few decades, we have been bombarded with
organizational theories: time and motion studies, job enrichment,
MBO, Theory Z, quality circles, self-managed teams, excellence,
TQM, empowerment, motivation, and one-minute everythings.
What generally happens is that an organization hears about a
theory they believe has been effective somewhere and they say,
"That's what we need . . . let's implement that here." Everyone
scurries around putting up posters and making announcements.
Several weeks or months later, the boss looks at the numbers and
says, "This new-fangled management theory isn't working . . .
scrub it." The posters come down and the announcements stop . . .
a brutal assault on morale and results.

There are two possible explanations:

- ❐ the new theory was wrong
- ❐ the implementation was wrong

Without evidence to the contrary and because the boss
didn't understand the most fundamental law of human nature, he
assumed his implementation was right and the theory was wrong.
Because we haven't understood the basic law of human nature, we
consistently throw the good out with the bad. The problem with
the management theories we've tried generally hasn't been the
theory, even when the theory wasn't perfect, . . . it's been the
implementation. But, because we didn't understand the laws
involved, we didn't know what to fix. We didn't know whether to
jump off the cliff or look for a different dinosaur dinner.

Think about it. Few organizations deliberately fail. Even
the most belligerent, obtuse, cantankerous managers in the world

want to succeed. So if they knew a theory would bring them success, they would adopt it. And, if their implementation didn't work the first time, they would keep trying new ways to make it work . . . because they were certain it would work if they could just implement it properly.

I

It's as if you went out one cold morning and your car wouldn't start. You wouldn't throw it away. You'd call a mechanic to fix it because you know it started yesterday and you understand that something must be broken. But, if a stranger brings you a black box and tells you that it will make gold and you push all the buttons and pull all the levers and nothing happens, you will probably assume the stranger was a con artist and toss the black box in the local Dumpster.

The Blinding Moment

So, finally, we're getting to our epiphany: if we knew a management theory was right, we'd work with it until we got it right. And, in order to know if a management theory is right, we have to understand the basic law of human nature. Once we understand that law, we will know when a theory is right and we will know when the implementation is faulty.

Grow or Die*

What is this all-powerful, basic law of human nature? According to George Land in his book *Grow or Die*, it is simply this: the most fundamental drive of human nature is growth. When we are not growing, we are dying. (Although there are natural dormancy periods where growth is not evident.) This may sound trivial or obvious but we believe that not understanding this fundamental principle of human nature is the root cause of most organizational problems.

The destiny of all living things and all groups of living things is to reach out and affect ourselves and our environment by absorbing materials and transforming them into extensions of ourselves. We do this by eating and drinking, by absorbing information about everything around us, and by exchanging information with others. The higher the "nutritional" value of our

---

* For readers who are biologists, "grow" is used in place of the more accurate term "transform."

I

environment, the more we grow physically, mentally, emotionally and spiritiually. And, if positive growth is frustrated, we will find self-destructive, cancerous ways to grow or we will wither and die. Our lack of understanding of this basic need to grow is sucking the life out of people in our schools, our businesses, our churches, our communities, and our nation.

The Thinking Environment Framework

The chapters in this section present the environmental framework necessary to support the growth that leads to organizational transformation. The first chapter explains the process of growth in organizations . . . the three forms of growth, how to encourage growth, and how to remove barriers to growth. The second chapter demonstrates how transformation comes exclusively through people and gives ideas for putting people first. Chapter 3 explains co-active ways to make your communication processes support transformation.

The focus of the entire book is growth . . . mental development of individuals and teams within organizations. Kate Ludeman in her book *Worth Ethic* cites a Public Agenda Foundation survey of working Americans which states that less than *25% of workers feel they're working at their full potential.* Think of what we could do with that untapped potential! . . . the schools we could build . . . the homeless we could feed and shelter . . . the diseases we could cure . . . the crime we could prevent. Think of what that wasted potential could mean to your organization . . . increased sales . . . lower costs . . . better customer relations . . . improved morale . . . new products . . . new markets . . . growth . . . increased profits.

When an organization commits to creating an environment which stimulates the growth of everyone in the organization, amazing things start to happen: ideas pop up everywhere, people start to work together instead of "playing politics"; new opportunities appear; customers begin to notice service and attitude improvements; collections of individuals begin to coalesce into teams. The very same environment that fosters peak performance in the individual is the environment that's necessary for peak team performance and organizational transformation. This environment isn't some kind of miracle that was only available in the early days of the space program, or to the Macintosh computer team, or the Disney World planners. This environment has been created in whole or in part by hundreds of organizations — Herman Miller, Stew Leonard's World's Largest Dairy Store, Ben & Jerry's, The Body Shop, Springfield ReManufacturing Company, Saturn, Patagonia, Kinko's, Motorola, GE, Merck, Disney, Federal Express, all the winners and all the runners-up to the Malcolm Baldrige Quality Award, and hundreds of other organizations, big and small, too numerous to mention.

I

It's not easy to create a transformation environment and it's all too easy to let it die. Despite its technological success, Wang Laboratories never had it; IBM had it but misplaced it; GM created it in its Saturn plant but is now "tinkering" with it; Sears didn't think it was important; and People Express created it magnificently but couldn't keep up with the growth it produced.

With today's environment of massive change, any company that thrives for long has to be striving to foster an environment of growth and transformation. Watch any company that is becoming more successful and notice the changes they're making. Somehow, someway they are fostering the growth of their people. In the following chapters you will learn how you can begin to create an environment that produces growth and transformation.

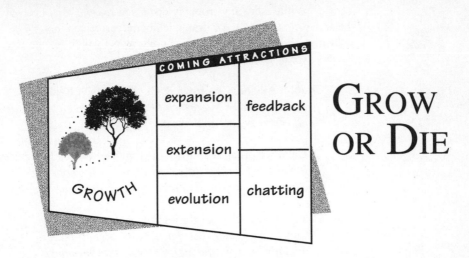

CHAPTER 1

COMING ATTRACTIONS

expansion · feedback

extension

evolution · chatting

GROWTH

GROW OR DIE

This chapter is dedicated to George Ainsworth Land whose book **Grow or Die,** *linking the biological facts of growth to the psychological process of human and organizational life, burned away layers of fog to reveal many truths.*

In 1981, Branch Banking & Trust of Wilson, North Carolina, held assets of $1.4 billion. Ten years later their asset base had grown to almost $7 billion. *Why?* In a turbulent decade of financial industry failures and scandals, how did BB&T's asset base increase by a factor of five?

Reflexite Corporation is a Connecticut-based company with a difference. In the five years between 1986 and 1991, sales for this technology-based company that competes head-on with 3M doubled and redoubled while profits went up six-fold. *Why?* Why has Reflexite done so well when the plant next door, the now defunct New Britain Machine, sits empty?

In 1983, Springfield ReManufacturing Company, a remanufacturer of engines, had a stock value of ten cents and a debt level 89 times its asset base! Ten years later the stock value is close to $20 per share and the company has reduced its debt ratio by over 4000%! *Why?* How did this low-technology company with no patents or proprietary products create wealth at a rate faster than almost all of the "glamour" stocks?

GROWTH

While there are probably dozens of reasons why each of the above companies have dramatically outperformed their industries and peers, the following comments by their respective leaders give us some insight:

❑ John Allison, Chairman & CEO of Branch Banking & Trust: *BB&T's biggest challenge is to provide room for all of our people to grow.*

❑ Cecil Ursprung, President of employee-owned Reflexite: *If you give workers some power, they will repay the company a thousand times over in performance.*

❑ Jack Stack, CEO of Springfield ReManufacturing Company: *When you appeal to the highest level of thinking, you get the highest level of performance.*

What's going on here? Are these "captains of industry" really focusing on staff growth, worker power, and levels of thinking? Yes . . . and these are only three examples in a growing field of transformed organizations. More leaders are recognizing the importance of the human element in organizations . . . and are beginning to do more than give the concept "lip-service."

We've talked about our "human resources" for decades and invested a great deal of time and effort trying to find the secret to motivation and organizational success. Most paths seem to lead toward a management style that is participative and democratic but we're not sure why. It seems like a good idea but is it really more effective? And, if it is, why is it more effective?

❖
Life Requirement:
Growth

George Land suggests a simple answer: *It's the only way to keep people alive.* It is a biological imperative that we grow or die. If we aren't growing, we're dying. An organization can be simplistically defined as a group of people trying to do something together. Therefore, the only way an organization can sustain growth is if its members are growing.

Growth is defined as the process that occurs when we reach out to our environment, take in nutritional materials and reformulate them until they become part of our selves. The cell does this by ingesting nutritional material from the environment and transforming it into new cells that match its own genetic pattern. Mentally we do it by absorbing informational material and using that material to think, communicate, socialize, invent, create, build, destroy, play and act in a thousand different ways. Growth is a requirement of life. Long past the time when our physical growth ceases, our need for mental growth continues. There is no such thing as a long-term, viable status quo.

GROWTH

Three Types of Growth

In order to create an environment that fosters the growth that leads to long term success and prosperity, we need to understand the three types of growth: Expanding - Extending - Evolving.

> **Expanding** — an increase in size without a basic change of nature. All organisms go through this stage of getting bigger, reaching their mature size. A giant redwood may grow to 400 feet while a petunia reaches only a few inches. Expansion is about growing to our genetically determined size — physically and mentally.

> **Extending** — an organism extends itself by reproducing or joining with similar others. At some point in its growth cycle, an apple tree stops getting bigger and begins to produce apples; a child reaches adult size and passes into puberty. In order to survive, all organisms find a way to biologically reproduce themselves. We humans also extend ourselves by connecting with friends, family and organizations. We choose people and groups that are like ourselves in some way and these groups become an extension of our self.

> **Evolving** — the gradual change over time toward a more complex and better adapted form. This often dramatic change comes through interaction with other organisms and the environment by way of mutual exchange of information. There is a search for possibilities, a willingness to push back apparent boundaries and become something new. Examples in nature abound: from the hummingbird that develops an extended bill used for retrieving nectar from deep flowers to the walrus with its massive layers of fat that helps it survive its arctic home to the organization that changes its strategy and "reinvents" itself.

GROWTH

George Land and Beth Jarman, in their book *Breakpoint and Beyond*, describe three phases of growth as Forming-Norming-Fulfilling.

> **Forming** is a a disorderly probing and exploration in order to find a unifying pattern.
> **Norming** is an orderly building on that pattern.
> **Fulfilling** requires a breaking of the original pattern in order to achieve full potential.

Between each phase is a "breakpoint" – a period of fundamental change which requires a shift in basic thinking patterns and altering of our world view (shared assumptions about how the world works).

PONDER BREAK

> *Think about your current personal growth. Which phase is most predominant for you? What supports your growth? What hinders it?*

The three types or phases of growth can be compared in terms of maturity or world view as follows:

Me/Mine — In the expansion stage the infant is only interested it itself. The child's job is expanding physically and mentally . . . making a bigger footprint in the world. Only disease or a malfunction in the physical or mental make-up prevents us from completing this stage and moving to the next.

Our Gang/Our Turf — At puberty, growth moves into extension . . . a search for connection by reproduction or finding others who are similar to us. This "teenager" state is ruled by peers and hormones and is seductive. It seems more comfortable than venturing beyond the familiar turf into the unknown arena of the next stage. Gangs, pregnant teens, racism, sexism and wars are some of the negative effects of getting stuck at this stage.

The Global Us/World System — The third phase of growth comes as we begin to value diversity and the mutual benefit that comes from sharing, appreciating and using the wide variety of information available to us. In this stage we recognize the need to find new sources of information beyond those on our own turf. When we find these new sources of information, we begin to become more than we were (although still within the boundaries of our genetic potential) as we incorporate the diverse information offered by others and the environment. Evolutionary growth requires a letting go of previous assumptions and comfort levels. It is a disruptive, chaotic stage . . . a time when the caterpillar crawls out on a limb, wraps itself in a dark cocoon and hopes for the best. People need all the help and support they can get at this stage.

GROWTH

While these types of growth provide a nice, neat breakdown for discussion, in actuality growth is not a simple, straight-forward process. Most people experience all three types of growth and all three forms are critically important. This is not a personality typing model where someone winds up saying, "Oh, I'm an Evolver . . . you're just an Expander." These are forms of growth that we each experience and each type needs to be fostered a great deal more than we currently do.

The Human Animal

Somewhere in our evolution — call it divine intervention or the next step in the "Grand Design," or will, or whatever — we made an evolutionary leap. This new wrinkle in our DNA made creativity possible. Not only made it possible, but made it a mandatory part of our growth process. Never before, in the world as we know it, was an organism granted the awareness and abilities needed to make such intentional and fundamental changes in its environment. While beavers might dam a creek, man was given the ability to conceptualize and implement the damming of great rivers to harness their power to light up the night. Man was given the ability to drastically change the natural order of things ... sometimes with dire consequences.

It was as if someone gave us the keys to the kingdom and said, "Ok, see what you can do with it." If you have a spiritual bent, you might believe that the use of creativity is a test — if we handle this drive and grow well enough, maybe we will make another evolutionary leap. It may be that the rapid change we're experiencing right now is the pot heating up getting ready to explode into a new realm. The result might be a new being that is as different from us as we are from the dog asleep on our hearth.

As our DNA pulled us into creativity, we required increasing amounts of information. The need to create made us look in new places for answers to the problems that surrounded us. And, the information we found showed us even more new

GROWTH

places to look and other new ways to change our environment which again created new problems and further sources of information and additional ways to change the environment . . . and so on.

Following the pull of our newly found creativity, we learned to exchange information with others and incorporate their learnings while at the same time sharing our learnings with them. Everyone benefitted ... families, tribes, organizations, and communities.

Creativity: Positive or Negative?

The growth process relates directly to our drive to create. Too often we talk about creativity as if it were a quality that we were either given or denied. It is not a talent or a personality quirk, it's the fundamental fact of human nature. The growth process involves taking in material or information from our environment and then doing something with it. We transform it into something new. If it's food we're absorbing, we create new cells. If it's information, we use it to create ballet, books or bridges ... or bombs.

Creativity itself is not linked to one type of growth — it's simply the way we translate who we are into external reality. Once creativity was added to our bag of tricks, it became available to us at every stage of our growth. A child may put information together in a new way to create a game as 8-year-old Joshua White did when he invented Dino-mite, a board game about dinosaurs. A different child might use his creativity to eliminate a frustration by killing his frustrator, as did a recent 12-year-old who shot a loved and respected store owner for a bicycle. A teenager might combine concern about his world with a new music style and come up with rap. Or a fanatical leader obsessed with protecting his turf could be very destructively creative about waging war.

Creativity is neither positive nor negative . . . it is a neutral tool for changing our environment. A bulldozer can be used to clear a space for a new health facility, level an old growth forest or destroy a church. A bulldozer is a bulldozer . . . creativity is creativity. How we use it is our choice.

The choices we make depend on our stage of growth and

whether our growth process is being frustrated or encouraged. A person with a supportive background who receives the nourishment necessary for growth will naturally grow into the evolution stage. On the other hand, an acorn might be bursting with life but if it happens to land in the middle of a four-lane highway, it's probably not going to fulfill it's potential.

GROWTH

How do you exercise your creativity? How do you translate who you are to the world around you?

Here is a brief description of how to nourish each "stage" of growth:

Expansion — basic physical needs must be met: food, shelter, clothing, security. Mental expansion comes from free availability of materials and experiences. This is the "dry sponge" stage. The environment should be rich with information that stimulates all the senses. When parents place a brightly colored mobile over a baby's crib they are increasing the nutritional growth value of that infant's environment. When people attend training programs, the information level of their environment is increased.

- ❒ **Nourishers:** Sensory stimulants such as music, color, texture, tastes, shapes, books, games, toys, magazines, animals, field trips, training sessions, nature hikes and other experiences.
- ❒ **Barriers:** Poverty, disease, inadequate education system, warfare, sterile environments, monotonous routines, low self-esteem, dysfunctional families, lack of support or encouragement.

Extension — needs for affiliation and connection must be met through interaction with other people and identification with groups and organizations.

- ❒ **Nourishers:** Social events, group projects, plays, readings, recitals, dances and meetings, common eating areas, central water coolers, accessible conference rooms, newsletters, e-mail, telephones, faxes, organization t-shirts, buttons, bumper stickers, stationery, business cards, uniforms, membership cards.
- ❒ **Barriers:** Chain of command communication structure, excessive rules or bureaucracy, rigid

GROWTH

organizational charts, favoritism or cronyism, walls or barriers between people, enforced silence or excessive noise levels that prevent interaction.

Evolution — Willingness to change and reach the outer limits of our potential combine with our need for self-actualization and service. We must have a high level of exchange of information between ourselves and diverse groups and the environment. There needs to be a safe environment for change and experimentation.

❏ **Nourishers:** Interaction between diverse groups, field trips, job exchanges, cross training, cross-functional teams, tolerance of mistakes, support for risk taking.
❏ **Barriers:** Bigotry in any form, pyramidal hierarchies, restrictions in communication flow, lack of organizational direction and vision, harsh punishment of mistakes.

PONDER BREAK

Is your organization nourishing the growth of every individual? Are any of the growth barriers evident in your group, team, department, family, church, school, community? How can you begin to get rid of them?

The Growth Model

There is a relatively simple model of growth that we need to understand in order to foster growth in our organizations. The three steps are:

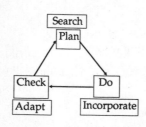

1. Searching — Looking for and finding material or information for growth. Requires nutrition and information.
2. Incorporating — Using the material or information for growth activity. Requires empowerment and freedom to act.
3. Adapting — Evaluating the effects of the growth activity and making necessary adjustments. Requires feedback.

Simplified even further, this is the Plan-Do-Check cycle. For hundreds of years we spent our time *doing* without much *planning*, then we developed a bunch of business schools to help us learn to plan. But we still haven't made enough progress on

GROWTH

checking. Most of us would really like to know how we're doing (if someone could tell us in a nice way, of course) but we resist like mad telling other people how they're doing. Even when we were shown how to do one-minute reprimands and praisings, we found it hard to do. Most of the magic from the total quality management programs comes from the emphasis on checking. TQM's frequent and regular data gathering and measurement provides a steady stream of feedback.

The process of growth involves finding nutrition or information, doing something with it, and then seeing how the environment reacts. If something positive happens, we know that what we did was a good thing and we can do it again or build on it in our future learnings. If something negative happens, we know we need to make an adjustment. If nothing happens, our learning is interrupted.

Feedback

❖

Job satisfaction depends on feedback.

Gary Bergerer, vice president of International Survey Research in Chicago states that in 1,990 attitude surveys of over 6,000 managers and 25,000 employees, feedback about employee performance was rated as one of the most important factors in job satisfaction. More than 60 percent were unsatisfied with the feedback they received.

In the growth process, negative feedback is actually better than no feedback because it provides more information about our actions. In most organizations, however, the environment provides little feedback, positive or negative. Even when there is a relatively high level of vocal "strokes" of the "nice job" variety, there is usually little real feedback. In order for the feedback to be effective, it needs have the following qualities:

❖

Feedback is more than "vocal strokes."

 real time — feedback must be received as soon as possible after the action. What normally happens is *plan-do-* . . . *(elapsed time)* . . . *check*, by which time everyone has forgotten what it is we're checking.

❏ **on-going** — it must be part of an on-going process so the person has a chance to make revisions, a chance to "redo" and improve — the growth cycle becomes plan-do-check—*plan-redo-check*-etc. What we often call feedback is actually a grade. Turn in a project, get an A or an F, pass or fail, win or lose. No chance for rework,

GROWTH

no chance to try again. *The passion for learning is stoked by feedback and killed by grades.*

❑ **meaningful** — the feedback must contain information. Comments such as: *Good job* or *You screwed up the count again* don't provide enough information to adjust actions. Meaningful feedback is specific: *I really like the way you organized the shelves so it's easier to reach the faster moving items . . . It looks like the count is off — did you check the supply room and the holding area?*

❑ **accountable** — feedback should guide behavior relative to the goals and objectives of the group or organization. *Your arrangement of the shelves is going to help us reach our goal of same-day shipments . . . Double checking invoices has cut our billing errors but it's taking twice as long to get them in the mail . . . can we find a way to speed up the process without losing accuracy?*

PONDER BREAK

When was the last time you received, or gave, feedback that met all four of these criteria?

Encouraging Innovation

For the past decade there has been a lot of discussion about Japanese vs. American productivity. The Japanese invented the word for continuous improvement (kaisen) while we acted like we were somewhat handicapped in the worker motivation category. According to this belief, Japan had people who worked hard and did all that quality stuff and we just had people who wanted to punch the time clock, collect their checks and go home. One of the statistics used to support this hypothesis was the staggering numbers of suggestions-per-employee that Toyota and other Japanese firms experience versus our rather pathetic record.

❖
Suggestion usage:
Japanese 95%
Americans 5%

In recent years, we've done a lot to stimulate employee suggestions but we have been far less effective at implementing those ideas. And, the key lies in the implementation. Recent analysis states that Japanese firms implement 95 percent of the suggestions received while American firms implement only 5 percent of their employee suggestions. Why would anyone make a suggestion if there was a 20 to 1 chance that it wouldn't be implemented?

One firm in our not-so-distant past had an official suggestion policy (it was in the Employee Handbook) and nice wooden boxes in three or four locations around the building. The boxes were locked and when we tried to check for new suggestions, we discovered that the keys had been lost years ago! How many hapless employees had naively stuffed their ideas into that locked abyss and then anxiously awaited some feedback? How many times would the average, idea-filled employee offer his suggestions to those official-looking boxes before he figured out that there was a major gap between policy and reality?

GROWTH

Not all American companies are lax in responding to suggestions. IBM acknowledges all suggestions and estimates that employee suggestions saved the company over $300 million in the four-year period from 1978-82. Total Quality programs have been extremely effective at raising the awareness of the potential benefits of suggestion programs and the importance of recognizing and implementing suggestions in companies across the nation.

One example of a company that does an excellent job of stimulating and acting upon employee suggestions is Reflexite. CEO Cecil Ursprung charged Matt Guyer, manufacturing manager, with developing a feedback loop where suggestions didn't get lost, one that didn't duplicate the existing structure for getting things done in the company. Guyer brought representatives together from various departments for a day to reinvent a suggestion program.

The resulting program was the Employee-Assistance Request System (EARS). But this wasn't just another passing program. Every employee attended classes to learn the steps and skills necessary to identify and solve problems. The EARS process gives them a way to identify problems, document them and plot and evaluate potential causes. It also provides them with a process to determine costs and benefits of solving the problem.

Within 24 hours of receiving a suggestion, the EARS coordinator assigns an action coordinator who immediately contacts the originator. Together, they fill out as much of the form as possible, work through the problem solving steps and decide if they will need a team. They develop a solution and determine a follow-up date to verify that the solution is working. Two weeks after that, the EARS form is distributed to top management, who visit the EARS originator and discuss the project. Shortly thereafter the originator receives a certificate of appreciation.

"EARS works," explains Guyer, "by making people who identify problems step back and quantify the magnitude of the problem and its impact on the entire company before offering a solution. That allows them not only to offer better solutions but also to understand why some problems are given a higher priority than others."

❖

Feedback is our guidance mechanism.

When the growth drive is not frustrated, people want to improve their environment; they want to make products better; they want to offer better customer service; they want to have a more pleasant working environment; they want to cut costs. Without proper feedback, however, they aren't sure which direction they're going. Feedback is how they know they're on track or off. What employees object to most is simply not knowing.

What do you do to make sure ideas are listened to and acted on — not only at work but at home and in all of the organizations you are part of?

Change and Stress

> **Calvin:** *I thrive on change.*
> **Hobbes:** *You?! You threw a fit this morning because your mom put less jelly on your toast than yesterday!*
> **Calvin:** *I thrive on making **other** people change.*

Thanks Bill Watterson, cartoonist extraordinaire. Obviously Calvin went to the same business school as many other managers. Probably the number one word in management literature today is change. We've heard it described a hundred different ways and all of them boil down to fast and chaotic.

❖

Uncertainty = Stress

The ongoing debate about change though is whether people hate it or love it. We seem to love the part of change that gives us a chance to grow and explore new avenues. We love buying new cars, exploring exotic vacation spots, wearing new clothes, and having the latest electronic gadgets. We hate the part that threatens our security. We hate wondering whether we'll have a job once the smoke clears, not knowing whether or not we'll be able to "make it" in the new environment, and not knowing if we'll have friends in the new group. What we really hate is the *uncertainty* of the change . . . the feeling of having no control.

GROWTH

The breakup of AT&T has been described as one of the most significant planned organizational changes of the twentieth century. The breakup created a high level of stress among employees who had thought they had a "job for life." Suddenly, they were "Ma Bell's orphans," abandoned by the company that had traditionally provided career-long caring and support.

Susan J. Ashford, associate professor of organizational behavior in the School of Business Administration at the University of Michigan, studied the AT&T break-up to gain information about the effectiveness of various strategies used for coping with stress during this change.

One of Ashford's findings reinforced previous studies that cited uncertainty as the prime cause of change-related stress. Most transitions are accompanied by uncertainty about procedures and the impact to daily routines and careers. Employees are uncertain about terminations, transfers, new supervisors, new policies, and possible new demands. Will they be able to meet the new requirements? Will they prosper under the new conditions. Feelings of competency are suddenly disrupted and employees lose their sense of control.

Employees who can maintain a sense of competency and feelings of control, at least partially, seem to suffer less stress than those who do not experience those feelings. Self-esteem buffers the employee from the ravages of the uncertainty associated with change. Ashford's studies also found that employees who have a relatively high tolerance for ambiguity experience less stress.

The Power of "Chatting"

One surprising result of Ashford's study was that some commonly used "change techniques" actually increased stress and the one that relieved stress the most was simply "chatting." She looked at techniques such as perceiving the change as a challenge, ignoring the situation, trying to find out more about the change, asking for feedback and expressing feelings. The techniques that

Openly discussing feelings reduces stress.

GROWTH

tended to mask feelings, such as looking at the change as a challenge (called "putting on a happy face"), didn't work. The method that most often succeeded was open expression of feelings . . . "chatting" about the change and sharing fears and concerns. Openly discussing concerns helped reduce the stress prior to the transition and was shown to have lowered stress levels for six months following the change.

This study indicates that the most important thing a manager can do in a transition period is allow employees to express their feelings. It seems to be even more important than providing them with information about the change although that is a critical second step. Establishing a climate where employees can "chat" freely and vent their concerns greatly reduces stress and smoothes the transition even when the concerns are not alleviated.

Employees need to share their worries and concerns and know that those concerns are taken seriously. Without official permission to share their concerns, employees usually feel that they have to appear positive in order to get management approval. When they can express their feelings openly, the stress of maintaining a "front" is removed. Even if management can't remove the concerns, employees feel listened to and valued.

PONDER BREAK

What changes are going on in your group that people might want to "chat" about?

Building Walls

Marvin Weisbord begins his outstanding book *Productive Workplaces* with a story from his past. It was the mid-60s and he was working in the printing/direct mail business his father had founded. Weisbord was fairly typical of managers during that time — everything he knew about management came from doing rather than books or workshops. When he became interested in the possibility of using incentives to increase production, a friend of his introduced him to McGregor's *The Human Side of Enterprise* (the management Theory X/Theory Y book).

Weisbord immediately recognized that he wanted to be a "Theory Y" manager but when he looked around him he saw "Theory X" stuff: "time clocks, narrow work rules, jobs so

GROWTH

subdivided anyone would be bored, grown people treated like children, never let in on decisions, given no consequential information about the business or even their own work, expected to deliver for management and not to reason why, all in return for a $5 raise every six months, a turkey at Christmas, and a chance, if they didn't die of boredom in the meantime, to become supervisors."

Weisbord decided to change his style of management. One of the first requests he received was for a wall down the center of the large order processing area. The billing people and the order entry people didn't like each other and the supervisors thought it would end the fighting if they couldn't see each other. In keeping with his new Theory Y management style, Weisbord built them a wall.

Order processing was organized on a typical functional basis with no cross training. Any time someone was absent, that person's function went undone and progress was halted; since turnover and absenteeism were high, the department was often backlogged. Weisbord's first action was to reorganize the department into work teams, each handling a block of customers with each person on the team able to handle all the tasks required by the team. The new teams were formed including one person from each of the former functions and instructed to teach each other their jobs. Supervisors become floating coaches.

The first result was chaos. Problems came up that people didn't know how to handle . . . problems that had always been handled by supervisors or higher management. A weekly meeting was instituted to work through all the problems. Weisbord describes the meetings, "The meetings dragged on interminably. I could not believe that such a little business could generate such a long list of problems, or that so many people knew so little about what they were doing — including me. I realized with a pang that the supervisors, now eliminated, had for years been making every decision. Every one, that is, except those (and I suddenly was appalled by the number) that they used to delegate upward — to me."

After four of those "interminable" meetings, Weisbord decided that this experiment in work redesign was a failure. There were too many problems and the weekly meetings were taking too much time. He decided to announce the end of the experiment at

❖

Learning together takes time.

GROWTH

the fifth meeting. As the meeting opened, in an attempt to delay his announcement, he asked for problems. An embarrassed silence followed.

Finally, one woman said, "We don't have any this week." Sensing Weisbord's surprise they told him they had learned how to handle all the problems from the other meetings! For Weisbord, the light dawned and he realized that the meetings he had thought a waste of time had actually been learning experiences for the team members.

Perhaps the biggest lesson from his first experiment in participative management came a week later when the teams called an ad hoc meeting and told him they wanted the wall taken down. When he asked why, they replied, "We don't need it anymore; we like talking to each other."

Weisbord summarizes his experience:

In a learning organization, of course, you don't need walls. When everybody has a chance to learn, grow, and achieve, when mistakes become okay, when a lot of people get in on the action there is a great deal more control in the system — self-control. It's the strongest kind, but it can't be bought, legislated, or behavioral-scienced in.

It's an ironic twist that the goal of almost all management systems — control — is only really achieved by turning control over to someone else. The harder we clamp down as managers, the more human nature oozes out from under. Take away the clamp and provide a guiding beacon and the ooze self-organizes and marches off in unison toward the goal. While the concept is simple and true, the implementation is complex enough to provide challenges for a lifetime.

PONDER BREAK

How does your organization try to "control" behavior and actions? Are the controls effective? Are they necessary? What might work better?

Chapter Mindmap

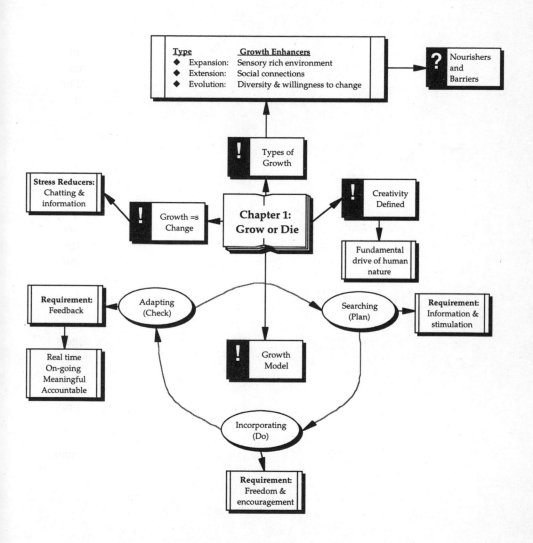

CHAPTER 2

The secret of education lies in respecting the pupil.
— Ralph Waldo Emerson

It was a time of magic and mayhem . . . a season of giants and legendary deeds. It was October 1988. The World Series had begun with 24 battered, bruised and aging Dodgers facing two dozen confident, muscular, young Athletics. The odds from Las Vegas were running heavily against the Dodgers and the experts said that this might be the shortest series in recent history. But, the games weren't played in Las Vegas nor in the columns of the sports pages. They were played on the green-grass diamonds of Los Angeles and Oakland. And there, something magical happened.

Las Vegas hadn't counted on an Orel Hershiser reaching a state of wizardry late in the season and hurling his magic through a series that included two shut outs and three base hits (almost unheard of for a pitcher). The sports writers had no way of knowing that a Kurt Gibson, limping on both legs, could get up in the ninth inning with the Dodgers down one run, two outs, the count 3 and 2, and hit the crucial game winning home run even though he could hardly make it around the bases. How could anyone assess the impact of a Mickey Thatcher, who thought his career was over but wanted to play so badly that he offered to play for the Dodgers' minor league team for free? A Mickey Thatcher who played every second with the abandon and enthusiasm of a little leaguer and astonished everyone when he hit two home runs in the series.

Magic happens frequently on baseball's field of dreams with millions of peanut- and-hotdog-stuffed fans watching avidly. But, it also happens privately, in the generally unnoticed halls of business. In certain circumstances, people go beyond their own wildest expectations to accomplish the undoable. What are the circumstances that kindle those sparks of magic?

A clue comes from Dodgers Manager Tommy Lasorda whose simple management philosophy didn't come from a text book. When Tommy was 15, he read a slogan on the top of a can of Carnation milk: *Contented cows give better milk.* Connecting that farm philosophy to the development of better ball teams, Lasorda has spent over forty years in baseball and is a three-time winner of the National League's Manager of the Year award. His attitude has also helped create one of the most popular clubs in the league. Dodger Stadium regularly sells its allotment of season tickets and has one of the highest attendance averages in baseball. The Dodgers manage to keep their players happy and that helps keep the fans happy. Seems simple, doesn't it? Again, the principle is, the implementation isn't.

The Big Four:
Respect-Trust-Commitment-Recognition

Federal Express built a new industry and gained recognition as the first service company to win the Malcolm Baldrige Quality Award with a company philosophy of: *People-Service-Profits.* They know their people have to come first or nothing else comes at all. By putting their people first they are able to deliver on their advertised promise: *Absolutely, positively, overnight!* ... on over a million pieces of mail and freight every working night.

What does it mean to put people first? Organizations are generally viewed as groups of people trying to do something . . . generally trying to do that something with limited resources . . . and doing it for someone else. Since the Industrial Age began, we've been tinkering with the elements of this process: people, resources, customers, products. We divided the group of people into managers and workers and developed various schools of thought on how to fix each. We assigned inspectors to check for quality and hired accountants to concentrate on our resources. Another group was assigned to customers and we called them salespeople and marketing or customer service reps.

All this looking at the pieces created a lot of motion and made work for a lot of consultants, but our organizations are still broken: families are labeled dysfunctional, schools aren't educating, governments are mired in gridlock and, in corporate America, the *Fortune 500* giants lost 4 million jobs in the 1980s!

We've looked at all the pieces, maybe it's time to look at the glue that holds them all together. By definition, an organization is not one person — it's a minimum of two. And it's not just any two people, it's two or more people trying to accomplish something. So it's not enough to look at the two people, we have to look at the space between them where their interaction takes place. As the ancient Sufi teaching says:

> *You think because you understand* one *you must understand* two*, because one and one makes two. But you must also understand* and.

Think of the relationship between you and one or more of your co-workers. Describe the relationship space between you. What strengthens it? What weakens it?

In organizations, the *and* is the interaction between people . . . the relationships. For the interaction to hold people together, to act as a "glue" for the organization, there must be four ingredients: respect, trust, commitment, and recognition. The stronger these elements, the stronger the bond between the people in the organization and the more successful the organization will be at accomplishing its goals.

Putting People First Starts with Respect

One of the latest management trends is outsourcing — subcontracting to other organizations for services or product components. Outsourcing allows an organization to concentrate on its core competencies and aggressively upgrade those activities. But a *Wall Street Journal* article covers the downside of outsourcing, stating, "Contracting out, the cost-cutting brainchild of the 1980s, is causing headaches among a loyal

booster, the steel industry." The article goes on to detail the corruption discovered in the contracting process for the outsourcing: kickbacks in the forms of cash, computers and equipment, and additions to private homes.

The boxed, highlighted summary of the article reads, "The process (of outsourcing) can improve flexibility and lower costs. But the process also transformed dozens of *low-level supervisors* (emphasis added) into power brokers, funneling multimillion-dollar jobs to favored contractors." A steel industry customer was quoted as saying, "The problem was people at the plant level had more power than they're supposed to."

Both of these quotes reflect a common, underlying philosophy about workers: they can't be trusted. It's the "us and them" mentality. We're the good guys and they're the ones that have to be watched. There are millions of examples of employee fraud and negligence that "prove" the truth of this mentality. What we seldom think about is how that way of thinking creates it's own reality. The thought process that says employees are dishonest, uninterested in the goals of the organization, lazy, incapable of higher level thought and decision-making produces an environment where neither "side" respects the other, a big-brother environment of inspections, audits, time clocks, and drug tests.

The quality movement recognized that quality could not be "inspected into" a product. Quality is a process that happens at every incremental step of production which means that every person involved with the process needs to be a quality producer and an independent quality inspector with the authority to do what it takes to insure quality. The leap required for movement into a quality environment isn't statistical process control or fishboning or creative problem solving . . . it's *respect for the individual employee*. Success or failure of quality and other productivity improvement programs hinge directly on this one human element. The realization that the fate of the company rests in the hands of each individual member of the organization is exceedingly uncomfortable and threatening for many managers and supervisors.

❖
Quality leap:
respect

That discomfort is easy to understand. Managers and supervisors have their jobs because of the belief that workers have to be "watched" and there are a lot of tasks that the rank-and-file

employee can't handle. The *Wall Street Journal* article shows only one example where management tried to implement a new policy to improve productivity but the "low-level" supervisors screwed it up. In this example, the belief that the rank-and-file couldn't be trusted led to the conclusion that management needed to take back authority and put it into the hands of professional subcontract managers.

That's the way the mentality works. However, in the specific example of outsourcing, the problem wasn't that the supervisors were trusted too much or that they had more power than they were supposed to have. It was that they *didn't have enough* power or trust or respect.

In one case a supervisor received a computer and office equipment from a contractor. There is at least a possibility that he needed the computer and equipment to do his job but there was some kind of bureaucratic cost freeze in effect so he went around the regulations and found a way to get what he needed. Of course, there's also the possibility that he wanted the stuff for his office at home because he's starting his own company. The long-standing management mentality states that "those people," the workers, will always cheat the company given a chance, if they're not closely supervised. The "new management" mentality says that in an environment of respect, trust and commitment, members of the organization are so aligned with the organization that "ripping-off" the organization would be the same as stealing from themselves.

It's obvious that the steel industry's new policy of outsourcing was not carried out in an environment of mutual respect and trust. Decades of labor unrest, downsizing, and plant closings had undermined morale. Union leaders saw outsourcing as another attempt to get around labor contracts, probably with some justification since USX wound up paying over half a million dollars in back wages for contracting out work that could have been done by existing employees . . . often at a lower cost.

The primary prerequisite for putting people first is respect. In an environment of respect there is a basic assumption that everyone in the organization is a responsible adult and each person is valued as an individual and as a vital part of the team. Each person is viewed as a partner who shares in the risks and the rewards and who cares deeply about the outcome of the

Little boxes are unhealthy places for people.

organization's endeavors. Each individual's need to grow and develop his unique potential is appreciated and the importance of the interaction between members of the organization is nurtured. People in little boxes can't produce the results that are needed for organizations to flourish in the Information Age.

What if organizations weren't hierarchical? What would a "boss" do?

What Does Respect Look Like?

There is a wonderful book about quality titled *I'll Know It When I See It, a Modern Fable about Quality* by John Guaspari. Like many organizational intangibles such as quality, respect is much easier to recognize when we see it and all too easy to notice when it's lacking. A story we heard recently happened in a national association headquarters. An employee went to the executive director asking to order paper clips . . . probably at the exact same time the director had been asked to reduce the budget by 15%. The harried director said that if the employees looked around their work areas and got "creative," they could probably find enough paper clips to avoid re-ordering. The director "challenged" the employees to spend 15 minutes finding as many paper clips as possible so they could avoid re-ordering. *Treating employees as though their time was less important than paper clips is not a demonstration of respect!*

Organizations that respect each member of the group often create different ways of addressing each other. The terms *associates, partners, members, co-workers, team members* often replace *employees, subordinates, hired hands, assistants, wage-earners, workers, or laborers*. There is a continuing effort to guarantee fair pay and benefits in accordance with community standards and with the company's ability to pay. Benefits are generally equally available to all. There is a noticeable absence of executive perks such as special dining rooms or reserved parking.

A well-known example is Patagonia, a successful ($100 million plus) outdoor clothing manufacturer in Ventura, California. Turn-over is almost non-existent at this company that religiously contributes 10% of annual pre-tax earnings or 1% of sales (whichever is larger) to environmental causes. Because the company appeals to young, outdoor enthusiasts who are in their prime child rearing years, Patagonia has established an on-site child development center which is viewed as a model for the future.

The offices at Patagonia are open bays designed to encourage interaction between people. The company's founder, Yvon Chouinard, has as his "office" a desk in the corner surrounded by the new product development group. While having the leader's desk in the middle of operations isn't mandatory for an organization to show respect for its people, it is an example of how barriers between management and the rest of the organization are eliminated. Other examples are common eating areas regularly used by the entire organization, open doors that are genuinely open to people at all levels, management by wandering around, and frequent and regular meetings of senior management with people from all levels of the organization.

Respect often shows up in the form of unique benefits or benefits that are unusual for a company's size or industry. Child care centers are no longer unique but George Tash's small plumbing-parts company in Moorpark, California, with only 30 employees took this benefit a step further and created their own private school. The G.T. Water Products elementary school is financed entirely by the company and is in an enclosed section of the firm's warehouse. The company matches its workday to the school day, which runs from 8 a.m. to 4:30 p.m. Instead of hopping on a school bus at the end of the day, the students commute home with their parents. This unusual benefit has almost eliminated employee turnover . . . and earned the company a slot on *Working Mother* magazine's list of the 60 best companies in the U.S. to work for.

Child care centers, on-site schools, elder care assistance programs, job sharing, flexible hours, and fitness programs are becoming common benefits. AT&T Universal Card Service (UCS) demonstrates some of the more unusual benefits such as using the term associates rather than employees, the availability of a 10-minute massage, a player piano in the dining room, spontaneous performance awards heralded by a fog horn, a "World of Thanks" board where associates express appreciation to each other, associate art work displayed on walls and a mini-mall which houses a company credit union, shoe repair, post office, florist and gift shop. UCS believes in giving people the extras in order to let them know how much they are needed.

Something must be working since UCS has not only experienced record-breaking growth but also won the 1992 Baldrige Quality Award. Perhaps the youngest company to win the prestigious award, UCS has only been in operation since 1989.

Benefits which show concern for the employee as a person pay off in much more committed employees and a turnover rate that is a fraction of those at similar companies.

How is respect shown for the individual members of your organization?

Emphasis on Training

Organizations that respect their people, consider them an asset. In the Information Age, brain power has replaced back-power. But brain-power is hard to see and measure. By the end of 1992, almost 3 million "obsolete" 386-based personal computers had been replaced by the faster 486s. Yet the same companies that are quick to upgrade equipment and computers often do little to upgrade their human capital. Even after a decade of touting the benefits of training, the American Society for Training and Development (ASTD) states that American companies are spending a marginal 1.4% of their payroll on training . . . and that training reaches *only 10%* of the workforce. Japanese and European-owned companies *based in the U.S.* spend three to five times more on employee training than American-owned companies.

Companies that are interested in transforming themselves are deeply committed to development of their employees. When James R. Houghton took over as Corning's chairman in 1983, he began at once to talk about the Corning of 1995. That was Houghton's target date for turning Corning into one of the world's 10 most admired companies. He wanted a company that was in the top quartile of *Fortune 500* companies for return on equity, one where Corning employees regularly met the quality standard of getting the job right "the first time, on time, every time," one that doubled or tripled current levels of productivity, and a company that had a strong representation of women, minorities and non-U.S. nationals throughout. The backbone of their transformation program was training. They launched a program designed to enable all employees to spend 5 percent of their working time in meaningful education and

❖

Corning goal: 5% of time spent in training for *all* employees

training by 1991. This commitment to employee development helped them achieve a consistently high growth rate and seven years of record earnings.

For years Johnsonville Foods has been a model of participative management. Written about in hundreds of business publications, in the early 80s this Sheboygan, Wisconsin, sausage maker decided to transform itself. One of the keys to their transformation process was a decision to change the focus of the company from using people to build a great business to *using the business to build great people*. One of the first things they did was change the name of the training department to the "member development department." Its focus broadened from training to all aspects of mental development.

In addition to formal training programs, the company sets aside $100 annually for each person to spend on personal development activities. Linda Honold, a partner in Leadership Dynamics, a consulting firm that is an offshoot of Johnsonville Foods states, "Members can spend the money for a book on sausage making, a class on personal computers, or even a magazine on deer hunting. The learning experience doesn't have to be work related, but it does have to encourage the person to think." The company stocks a resource center with books, audiotapes, videotapes, and magazines of interest to company members. Topics covered in the resource center include everything from how to write a business plan to scuba diving. Johnsonville has a generous profit sharing program which is paid out twice a year but they have learned a deeper lesson of motivation: money is what helps people get to sleep at night, not what makes them get up in the morning. Success and accomplishment (read: growth) are what really motivate people.

Prime motivator: growth

Tom Peters in his video, *Leadership Alliance*, celebrates the Johnsonville transformation describing the organization as one that moved from almost total dictatorship to one that has gone further than most other organizations in turning the reigns of control over to the employees. The bottom line of the transformation is a productivity level which has increased 300% and a ten-fold increase in sales. One of the most telling statistics is Johnsonville's complaint to compliment ratio. In the "bad old days" they averaged five complaint letters for every compliment letter. Today the ratio is 2.8 compliments for every complaint . . . an enormous positive shift, especially considering that people are much more likely to register complaints than compliments.

❖
Johnsonville transformation: Productivity up 300%!!!

What opportunities for training and development are encouraged by your organization? Are opportunities open to every person?

It's About Getting Better

Bruce Woolpert, CEO at Granite Rock tells his employees: *Focus every day on being better.* For companies that are committed to training and employee growth, the process of becoming smarter is just as important as the subject studied. Training can be provided in companies of any size. Here are a few suggestions:

❑ have weekly book discussions (suggested examples: *Total Customer Service, Kaisen, The Great Game of Business, Thinkertoys, Leadership and the New Science, The Fifth Discipline*)

❑ stock a library with the latest books, magazines, audio-tapes and videos and encourage employees to use the library

❑ encourage people who attend outside seminars to hold an in-house class to share the information

❑ sponsor in-house expertise-sharing sessions

❑ join with other small companies to purchase expensive training programs jointly

❑ ask employees what they would like to know — what would make their jobs easier and then design a course around that

❑ if you have an alliance with a larger company, they might be willing to share training materials

❑ community colleges generally have training programs that can be tailored to individual company needs

❑ make videos of certain processes and ask employees to brainstorm improvements

❑ invite business associates (lawyers, accountants, bankers, health care providers) to teach short in-house workshops

❑ offer advanced technical courses through National Technical University (NTU), a consortium of 45 leading engineering schools which delivers advanced technical courses and degree programs via satellite. Individuals or groups can achieve the highest quality education possible without leaving the work site.

What can you do today or this week to help your group (family, school, church, team, department) get better?

Continuous improvement is an excellent goal but too often we think of it as a process of improving the quality of products or service or as a way of improving specific procedures. Continuous improvement starts with improving the skills of people. Mike Plumley, CEO of Plumley Cos, an $80 million rubber company in Paris, TN, states, "Training employees was not something we decided to do out of the generosity of our hearts. It was something we needed to do to survive. The more we've been able to improve education, the better we've been able to manage our business."

Many organizations look at training as an expense and wonder how to justify it in a tight economy. But training can be a high pay-off activity. Corning requires a minimum 30 percent return on investment as a way of determining the highest priorities for training. ASTD estimates that the average return on investment for well-thought out training programs is 3 to 1. (Will Schutz, organizational development guru and developer of the "Firo" series of assessments, states that the return is more like 136 to 1!) Motorola calculates an even more impressive return on its employee training costs with some programs yielding as much as $33 in cash flow for every dollar spent.

   What might happen if you offered training to upgrade the skills of every member of your organization? How could you do it? How could you start with yourself?

Intellectual Capital

Every year colleges turn out thousands of bright young minds trained in accounting. Many of these ambitious accountants continue their study and undergo a rigorous testing process in order to earn the designation of Certified Public Accountant (CPA) or Certified Management Accountant (CMA). These highly trained professionals are charged with the responsibility for tracking the value of the organization's assets. And, they do an excellent job with furniture, equipment, vehicles, buildings and computers. But what about the organization's intellectual capital?

The importance of intellectual capital isn't limited to the likes of Apple, Intel, Microsoft and other high tech or research

45

firms. Granite Rock Company is a 400-employee producer of construction materials. In the 1980s the company realized that its quarry operations were becoming outdated and it began a complete modernization program which culminated in GraniteXpress, the construction industry's version of an automated teller machine. A driver inserts a card into a terminal, keys in the type and amount of rock he wants, and proceeds to the loading facility where his truck is automatically filled. GraniteXpress and the quality program that won the Baldrige Award for Granite Rock didn't come from management of the company's fixed assets . . . they resulted from the application of its intellectual capital. If a *rock quarry* has to manage its intellectual capital, what company doesn't?

Every company increasingly depends upon knowledge — patents, processes, management skills, technologies, and information about customers and suppliers. The sum of what everyone in the company knows which provides a competitive edge to your organization equals your intellectual capital. But, where do you find that on your balance sheet? Where's the management reporting system that gives you an idea of whether your intellectual capital is increasing or decreasing? Where's the strategic plan that tells you what intellectual capital you will need to meet tomorrow's goals?

❖ Is your intellectual capital increasing?

Dr. P. Roy Vagelos, CEO of Merck & Co., repeatedly voted one of America's most admired companies, stated in an interview with *Fortune* magazine: "A low-value product can be made by anyone anywhere. When you have knowledge no one else has access to — that's dynamite." Michael Tattersoll, president of the US office of Scientific Generics, emphasizes the importance of knowing what intellectual assets a company has. His consulting company helps firms identify skill sets and intellectual properties that have been developed but not commercialized. To demonstrate the potential financial impact of identifying and evaluating intellectual assets, Tattersoll describes the experience of one of his clients that was selling a segment of its business. An intellectual capital audit and evaluation increased the selling price from $90 million to $113 million!

For most companies, the management of intellectual capital is still uncharted territory. Pat Sullivan, president of Sullivan & Associates, a management consulting firm in Menlo

Park, California, says this area is like the elephant standing outside the door. We know it's there but we don't know what to do about it and we're not completely sure that we want it to come into the house. Sullivan states that we normally start our thinking at the back end of the process when we try to figure out how to make money with an intellectual property such as a patented product, copyrighted materials, or a trade secret process. Prior to having a tangible property, however, we start with an idea and we call those ideas intellectual assets. Continuing to back-up, we have unformulated ideas bouncing around in brains . . . this is intellectual potential or capability. The difficulty of evaluating or managing this potential starts to be apparent at this point because we are trying to measure or manage something that hasn't happened yet . . . some fuzzy potential. However, for knowledge-based companies that depend on generation and development of ideas, management of intellectual capital is critical to survival and valuation of intellectual property may soon prove essential to financial viability.

❖

How do you
measure
intellectual
potential?

Intellectual Capital Audit

American Airlines uses "generally accepted accounting principles" to indicate the asset value of its jetliners. However, the same accounting system treats the information system that runs Sabre, American's extremely valuable reservation system, as an intangible which doesn't show up on the balance sheet. While the accounting professionals wrestle with how to show the value of intellectual capital on financial reports, we need to think about how to manage those assets.

The first step in getting more from your intellectual assets, is to find them. Companies faithfully keep a listing of their fixed assets and their values but when a person joins a company he is given his position label and put into that box. If someone is a clerk in the accounting department, he is assumed to have math and clerking skills, period. People are a bundle of potentiality, some recognized and some unrecognized. That accounting clerk might have brilliant, unrecognized sales potential, or an inventive mind, or leadership abilities that would be lost to the organization without some form of intellectual capital audit.

Fred Altomare is an executive with IBM in northern California who ruefully tells about a job interview he had in the early 80s. It was with a new company with a powerful vision of

changing the world with computers. Fred was intrigued with their energy and commitment but eventually decided that it wasn't the right time for him to make a job change. However, he mentioned the start-up firm to his young secretary and a few months later she left to join them. Ten years later she retired from her job as vice president of marketing, one of Apple Computer's millionaires. Apple didn't see her as a secretary. It saw her as a person with many potential skills and gave her a chance to develop them and grow.

Transformation companies routinely hire from within. That process sets up a cycle where members are regularly reviewed to find the best candidate for an open position. People are frequently shifted from an area of recognized capability into a field of potential capability. Such shifts offer enormous growth opportunities.

If your organization depends on intellectual capital to create a competitive edge, you may want to begin to develop your intellectual capital asset system. The first step is to survey individual members of the organization. Here are question areas you might want to include in your survey.

❐ What are their job skills? (Rate each as to importance to job performance.)

❐ What skills do they have that are not being used?

❐ What are their hobbies?

❐ What are their special areas of interest?

❐ What are special study areas?

❐ What languages do they speak or read?

❐ What foreign countries or cultures are they familiar with?

❐ What skills or knowledge could they teach or share with others?

❐ How do they want to grow — what skills do they want to develop?

In an environment of trust and respect, this survey will uncover some potential skills that could be useful to the organization. However, in an environment that lacks trust and respect, this survey could be perceived as a "big-brother" attempt to manipulate people.

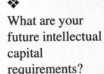

The other side of this intellectual capital audit is determining what intellectual capital and skills are critical to the organization. This will be different for each organization. It doesn't matter what the intellectual capital requirements are as much as that the prescribed set of skills and information is appropriate to the future growth of the company and that the total is increasing rather than decreasing. If Microsoft continues to develop its understanding of customer needs and programming and systems design, it increases its chances of continuing to stay ahead of the competition. If, for whatever reason, its intellectual capital should begin to decrease relative to the competition, the company will begin to falter.

❖

What are your future intellectual capital requirements?

Here are some questions to help you assess which skills and capabilities are critical to your future:

- ❏ What are the skill or technology elements of our product or service?
- ❏ Which skills or technologies make-up our "core competencies" and give us an advantage over our competition?
- ❏ What do we need to understand better than our competitors?
- ❏ What changes are likely to occur in the future and what knowledge base will be critical for coping with those changes?
- ❏ What knowledge or know-how have we developed?
- ❏ What skills are critical to each department's processes?
- ❏ How does each employee rate for each skill?
- ❏ What members of the organization could benefit from learning the skills or critical knowledge held by others?

How important is intellectual capital to your organization? What could you be doing to better identify and use those assets?

Respect in organizations is difficult to "see." It's more than pay and benefits. It's concern for the person and a recognition of how important every single member of the organization is to the whole. While it's hard to define respect, it's easy to recognize when it is not there: facilities that aren't clean, comfortable and safe; excessive executive compensation and perks; intimidating, bureaucratic or non-existent grievance processes; excessive control — time clocks, inspections of personal property or areas, drug tests, lie detector tests, etc. Sometimes the lack of respect shows up in more subtle ways. Recently we saw a dairy truck with a picture of a cow painted on the side. The caption above the picture read: *Our employee of the month — Bessie.* An advertising person's idea of a cute logo, but one that carries an underlying message that the best employee in the company is a cow!

Building Trust

It was a social gathering of top officers and their spouses, a self-congratulatory event until one person stepped forward and announced: *I think our quality stinks. Some of our competitors are much better and we ought to do something about it.* In many organizations, that comment would have created a breach between the company and the person making the brash statement. At Motorola, where this comment occurred and where dissent is nurtured, it prompted a series of discussions that resulted in Motorola's touted "six-sigma" quality program.

❖
Trust is built
on a foundation
of truth.

The basic building block of trust is truth. If members of an organization do not feel completely comfortable stating the truth as they see it, there is no trust. If they do not believe the organization tells them the truth, there is no trust. Truth within an organization means that no one "shoots the messenger," people are not asked to fudge reports or slant presentations, and information is presented honestly even when it may not be what people want to hear. A primary contributor to an environment of trust is a high level of corporate ethics within the organization and in its dealings with customers, suppliers and the community.

Some years ago a Colorado computer disk drive manufacturer was apparently having financial difficulties. In order to inflate sales and ease their financial pressures, the company reportedly began shipping bricks instead of disk drives. At the other end of the ethics spectrum, The Body Shop donates a

significant percentage of its time, efforts and money to help the natives of the South American rain forest. The computer disk drive manufacturer was rapidly draining its trust reservoir with its unethical, and illegal, activities. The Body Shop, on the other hand, fills its reservoirs by taking care of the environment as well as business. Corporate ethics may seem to be a fuzzy concept but it is one that more and more organizations are beginning to appreciate.

Larry Axline, president of Management Action Planning, Inc. in Ft. Collins, Colorado, specializes in corporate ethics programs. He defines ethics as the set of guidelines organizations use to decide and act. In most cases, ethical dilemmas involve people issues — *Are people being treated fairly? Is communication open and honest? How do we treat customers? . . . vendors? How do we resolve conflicts? Are we a good citizen, positively contributing to our community and the environment?*

Ethics is often viewed as a "soft" area — something that's important . . . something that we'll get around to . . . after we solve today's crisis. But, an organization's ethical standard based on shared values is actually part of the glue that holds the organization together. If people feel that they are being treated unfairly, morale goes down and with morale, productivity. When productivity drops, customers receive poorer goods and services which may impact the company's sales and profits. A downward spiral results in loss of sales, loss of profit and a further reduction of morale and productivity.

❖

Shared values bind us together.

Without the underlying trust that comes from establishing an ethical environment — open, honest communication, fair dealings for all stakeholders, and a system for resolving conflicts — most improvement programs will fail. In an environment of distrust, employees view quality, excellence, empowerment and other improvement programs of the moment as "whitewash" or manipulation. Without a solid base of trust, these programs are not only a waste of money, they irritate the employees and can cause a further drop in morale and productivity.

Organizational trust and ethics cannot be imposed or taught. Axline states, "It may not be possible, and probably isn't advisable, to teach ethics to adults. If people in the organization believe that their personal or spiritual beliefs are going to be challenged or coerced, they will understandably resist." The development of trust and ethics can be facilitated, however. People from all areas of the organization can be brought together to discuss ethics and the ethical dilemmas that face them. They can discuss the choices that are open to them in various situations. When an organization is committed to developing an environment of trust, truth and fairness, a series of workshop discussions can be effective at building trust between people.

One of the current organizational buzz-words is empowerment. However, it often seems to get more talk than walk. At one company we talked to, "empowerment" meant an employee could spend a*s much as $5* (!) trying to make a customer happy. What if a customer were $10 unhappy? At Franklin Quest, where customer service employees are empowered to "do whatever it takes" to make the customer happy, there are no artificially imposed limits and few rules. Franklin Quest is a Salt Lake City company specializing in personal productivity products and seminars. Franklin Quest's customer service department handles 30-40,000 calls per month and each service person has complete authority to handle the customer's concerns . . . their charter is to have a happy customer at the end of each call. Franklin Quest spends a lot of time training and sharing the company values with the service personnel but when the call comes in, it's the service rep's responsibility. There is a trust bond between the company and the service rep. The company trusts that the reps have the overall good of the company and the customer in mind and the service reps trust that the company will give them adequate training, back their decisions, and treat them fairly even if they make a mistake.

In an environment of trust, people say what needs to be said. In contrast, a study of the Challenger space shuttle disaster showed that there might have been as many as a thousand people who had doubts about the o-ring. Tragically, not enough of them trusted the system enough to voice their concerns and those who did speak up were not listened to. Trust is the second element of the organizational glue that holds people together, that keeps them going forward in their efforts to accomplish something together.

Commitment: Vision and Ownership

Pravda, one of the primary newspapers in the former Soviet Union, reported a story about a tractor repair factory. In the late 1970s the factory was completed in Siversk. It was a state-of-the-art plant with the capacity to repair 14,000 tractors per year.

The factory was hailed as a major component for improving the agricultural productivity of the region. In the former Soviet Union, projects were not often completed on time or as planned so the officials involved with this project were given high praise, medals and prestigious state congratulations as the project met planned milestones and deadlines. An older repair facility was torn down because it was obsolete and the new plant made it redundant.

There was only one problem with the Siversk tractor repair facility . . . *it did not exist!* Where there should have been a modern, busy factory there was actually only a collection of moldy, roofless buildings in a rubble-strewn industrial site hidden behind a solid fence.

Problems began at the start of the project and officials, unwilling to admit the truth, issued papers stating that progress was being made as planned. The lie grew and officials were bribed to sign off on each stage of construction. Paper progress looked so good that the project officials started to receive praise for their efficiency. Eventually the lie reached massive proportions . . . the toolworks didn't build the necessary equipment, fire and environmental inspectors signed off on the non-existent building, and other building inspectors certified that the plant met all the building codes.

The people building this plant weren't committed to improving the region's agricultural productivity . . . they were committed to protecting themselves from the wrath of Moscow. We talk a lot about commitment and vision in organizations but there is a fundamental truth that is often overlooked — *people are committed* . . . the real question is: to what?

Commitment to a common purpose points everyone in the same direction and transforms a collection of people into a motivated team with a goal. Commitment can't be purchased; it can't be forced or manipulated. But it is given freely when the vision of the organization aligns with the vision of its members and pulls them into action. In the past several years there has been much discussion about the need for corporate vision and mission statements. They're the first step in quality, customer service, and other organizational improvement programs.

Commitment is freely given when the vision of the organization aligns with the vision of its members.

Most mission statements are developed by the president or executive committee who generally lock themselves away in a

PEOPLE FIRST

conference room or go off on retreat to hammer out just the right words. While this is a noble sacrifice, it doesn't quite get to the crux of the matter. The primary reason for having a corporate mission statement is to develop commitment to the organization's goals.

Commitment is given by each member of the organization to the degree he or she is turned on by the mission statement. So the executives of XYZ Corporation go off on a corporate retreat and develop a mission statement that states that they will have excellent products and treat customers well. They send out copies of the statement to everyone in the organization and then sit back and wait for commitment to sky rocket. They may still be waiting!

❖

Does your mission statement have meaning?

Russell Ackoff in his insightful *Management in Small Doses* states: *Most corporate mission statements are worthless.* His main objections are that they consist largely of empty phrases (*excellence and quality*), often commit the organization to the obvious (making sufficient profits), or are operationally meaningless (offering the best customer service). JFK didn't suggest that the US develop a high quality space exploration system. He said let's put a man on the moon in ten years. A corporate vision needs to fire the imagination. It should be able to reach down through the organization and pull every member into action. It should make every member of the organization stand a little straighter and say, "I'm a part of that."

Polaroid recently decided that it's strategic plan wasn't guiding the company in the direction it needed to go. Senior management wanted to develop a new strategic vision that reflected the shared values of the entire organization and would, therefore, have a high probability of success. They expanded the strategic planning team from the few top executives to a group of ninety leaders of the company. The first step was to put all ninety members through a five-day workshop which dealt with leadership style and behavior. The workshop helped create a state of readiness for the planning process, a mindset for dealing openly and honestly with the tough choices ahead of them. For eight months after the workshop, the group worked on the questions about what kind of a company they wanted to create, what the dynamics of the market and the competition were, and what capabilities they possessed and what they would need to achieve their future goals. The strategic plan that emerged from this effort required a total reorganization of the company.

The more people involved in the development of the corporate vision, the higher the probability of that statement stimulating wide spread enthusiasm and buy-in. The vision statement needs to be a challenging statement of possibilities not just a rehash of platitudes. Ackoff's five guidelines for mission statement development are:

❖

Mission Statement 101:
More participation=
More buy-in

- ❏ It should contain a formulation of the firm's objectives that enables progress toward them to be measured.
- ❏ It should differentiate it from other companies.
- ❏ It should define the business that the company wants to be in, not necessarily the one it is in.
- ❏ It should be relevant to all the firm's stakeholders.
- ❏ It should be exciting and inspiring.

What is the vision held by your organization or group? Is it written? Does it stimulate commitment and enthusiasm? Does it challenge each member to grow and develop in order to achieve the vision?

Recognition: Ducks and Fun

Jack Kahl states that when he walks through the company doors at Manco, Inc., a Westlake, Ohio, manufacturer of packaging products and weatherstripping tape, he wants to find the same spirit and enthusiasm that someone would find in a family room. To make that happen at Manco, CEO Kahl created a corporate environment that builds commitment, enthusiasm and a sense of family. Manco has a fitness center that's open 14 hours a day, a pond out front, and a wooded area outside the cafeteria, complete with picnic tables and a walking trail. Employees place their personal slogans above their doors and have complete authority to stop production if they see something being made they wouldn't want in their own home.

Manco, with its $75 million in sales and 175 employees, has been employee-owned since 1985 and every member (referred to as partners) of the company knows how their company is doing. Goals are posted on bulletin boards throughout the company and daily sales, shipments and billings are shown on large wall-size charts in the cafeteria along with expenses and the monthly profit

❖

People first;
Customers second.

or loss numbers. Many people express doubt about the wisdom of sharing all that information with employees. Kahl replies, "You can't treat the customers well if you don't treat each other well first."

❖
Celebrate success or prepare for failure.

But Manco's environment is more than profit and information sharing and employee benefits . . . there's an atmosphere of fun. The company's smiling duck logo is everywhere (duck for *duct* tape!?!) and the pond in front of the facility has become a natural focus for "duck activities." Manco sponsors an annual "Duck Challenge Day." Internal partners as well as vendors and others associated with Manco set annual individual goals and challenges for themselves. People monitor their own performance throughout the year and then, based on how performance matches goals, each department chooses a person to be honored at the Duck Challenge. And, this is where you know you're dealing with a company of a different color. The people honored for their performances "get" to swim across the duck pond! According to Kevin Krueger, director of communications, last year 44 people swam across the pond . . . in 43 degree weather!

Another interesting thing about Manco's Duck Challenge Day is how they begin the ceremonies. In many ways it is a day to celebrate the successes of the previous year but Manco starts the day by recognizing its social obligation. It invites the community and educational groups that it supports and honors them first, presenting the company's donations to the groups so that the entire organization participates in the charitable process.

People need recognition for their efforts. They want to celebrate their successes. They thrive on being part of a winning team and grow when their individual efforts are recognized. Recognition doesn't have to be elaborate or expensive. Peer recognition can be more powerful than monetary awards. At Manco, people work hard to be able to swim across an icy pond — go figure! Recognition is an important part of the mysterious brew that holds us together and makes us want to accomplish the organization's goals as if they were our own, because, in fact, they are.

Putting people first in an organization is simple yet surprisingly challenging. Creating an environment of respect, trust, commitment, and recognition . . . an environment that allows personal growth to flourish . . . may seem like a fairly simple task and a basic concept of management. However, Wilson Harrell, CEO of a $500 million company discovered the hard way how important this concept is when he lost a $75 million subsidiary company through a messy unionization effort. In his book *For Entrepreneurs Only*, he discusses the events that led to the company's downfall and makes the following amazing statement:

> Back then (after the fall), I blamed a lot of people. On reflection, I was the real culprit. We had become a large company with a lot of people. And we were doing just what most big companies do: turning people into numbers. If I had known then what I know today, there is no way a union could have organized the company. If I had instilled an entrepreneurial spirit throughout the company; if I had encouraged creativity and allowed individuals to contribute; if I had recognized and rewarded entrepreneurial achievement; if I had allowed a sense of ownership to prevail and set our people free . . . then the need for protection would never have raised its ugly head, and there would never have been a union. But alas, I was just another big company CEO who got what he deserved.

How many management books talk about respect, trust, commitment and recognition?

For another perspective, check the index of all the management books in your library. How many of them list respect, trust, commitment or recognition as a topic of discussion? If your experience is similar to ours, you won't find many books that even mention these subjects.

How are the members of your organization recognized? Are they (and you) having fun?

Timeless Advice

Nothing we're saying here is new. It's as basic as time itself. Lao Tzu, a sixth century B.C. philosopher and author of the *Tao Te Ching* offered this advice:

A leader is best
When people barely know he exists,
Not so good when people
Obey and acclaim him.

Fail to honor people and
They fail to honor you.

But of a good leader
Who talks little,
When his work is done and
His aim fulfilled,

They will say,
"We did this ourselves."

Chapter Mindmap

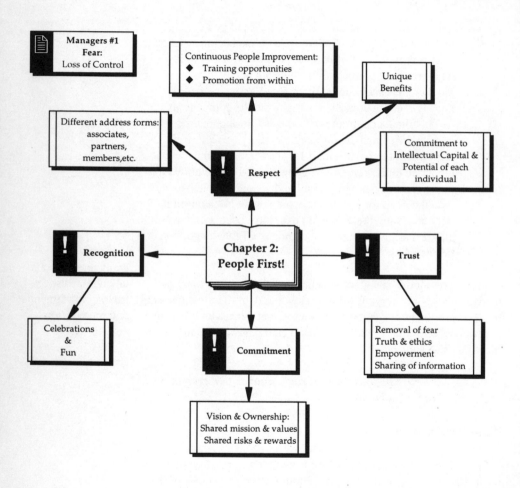

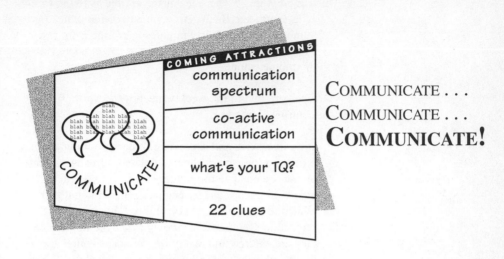

CHAPTER 3

COMMUNICATE . . .
COMMUNICATE . . .
COMMUNICATE!

We shall never be able to remove suspicion and fear as potential causes of war until communication is permitted to flow, free and open, across international boundaries.
— Harry S Truman

In conference rooms all across the country, usually about the third or fourth week of the month, the following scene plays repeatedly:

> The CEO and a few managers are sitting around the conference table when the controller walks in loaded down with computer print-outs and copies of last month's financial statements. After discussing all the pressing business, the controller is asked to discuss the numbers. She hands out copies of the statements and then puts up a copy on the overhead projector, apologizing for how hard it is to read the numbers. She starts to point out the change in sales from the prior month when the marketing manager says, "Hey, that figure for advertising can't be right! We cut back on advertising last month."

> The controller starts to thumb through the computer reports when the plant manager says, "You didn't get that rebate into last month . . . our supply cost should be

half what it is." The sales manager objects to the foreign sales figure and the meeting quickly disintegrates into number bashing. Thirty minutes later time is up and everyone goes back to work glad to forget about finances for another month.

Compare that to the weekly meetings at Springfield ReManufacturing Company:

Forty managers and supervisors enter a room where a profit and loss spreadsheet template is already projected on the screen. The room buzzes with activity then gets quieter as each manager begins to share the numbers related to his area of responsibility. The computer projection system makes it easy to see the numbers as they are entered and recognize variances which are discussed briefly. Arrangements are made to further discuss problem areas and at one point, Jack Stack, the CEO, asks a manager, "How can we help you?"

Numbers quickly fill the blanks in the spreadsheets and, within an hour and a half, the group has jointly developed the week's profit and loss statement, balance sheet and cash flow statement for eight business units. Announcements are made, a few jokes are cracked and the meeting ends. As the managers and supervisors leave, they pick up the printed copies of the financial statements they just generated and return to their groups where they will share the information gained, usually by the end of the day and in any event, no later than the end of the following day.

In 1979 Springfield ReManufacturing Company (SRC), located in Springfield, Missouri, was a dying division of a foundering giant. Losing $2 million on its annual sales of $26 million did not make SRC rank high with International Harvester, its parent company. Four years later, when IH expressed an interest in cutting the division loose, a foolhardy group of managers took the plunge and wound up "owning" a company with an 89:1 debt to equity ratio. A strong breeze would have put them out of business — and gale force winds are commonplace in the Midwest and even more frequent in industry.

The dreamer behind this daring venture was Jack Stack who believed in the company and its people. In order to buy SRC,

Stack and the 12 other managers who were attempting the leveraged buy-out needed to raise $9 million. From the beginning, they intended to make SRC an employee-owned company so they took their buy-out idea to the employees and asked for their investment. The 300 employees raised $67,500 — falling some $8.9 million short! Deciding that they hadn't explained the possibilities well enough, Stack called the employees back together and presented the plan and again asked for investment. This time the amount dropped to $65,000 — someone had rethought the plan and decided it was too risky.

In spite of Stack's extensive management experience, no one had taught him about profit or cash flow. But, he learned quickly as the buy-out group took their proposal to various lending groups where they were turned down 53 times. They soon learned how the financial world looked at numbers and ratios and they also began to understand how the numbers related to the work being done. Stack started to see the numbers as a way of keeping score in a game . . . the game of business. Stack also realized that there was no point in only one person or a small group of people knowing the score. In order to win the game, everyone had to know the score and how to play.

❖

Business Quandry:
Why do we keep
the rules and scores
a secret from the
players?

By 1993, SRC had eight separate business units, over 700 employees, close to $80 million in annual sales and a stock value that had increased from ten cents a share to $18.30 cents per share. The average employee equity in the company was over $30,000. Success didn't come from some innovative new product or process. As Stack states, "We didn't do this by riding some hot technology or glamour industry. Remanufacturing is a tough, loud, dirty business. Our people work with plugs in their ears and leave the factory every day covered in grease. What SRC remanufactures are engines and engine components. We take worn-out engines from cars, bulldozers, eighteen-wheelers, and we rebuild them, saving the parts that are in good shape, fixing those that are damaged, replacing the ones beyond repair. But in some ways engines are incidental to what we do. *Our real business is education.* (emphasis added) We teach people about business. We give them the knowledge that allows them to go out and play the Game." SRC defines their "game of business" as:

> *An open book style of management that gives everyone in the company a voice in how the company is run and a stake in the financial outcome, good or bad.*

In an interview with Stack, *INC.* magazine described SRC's management philosophy as, "so simple, so logical, so obvious that it was hard not to wonder, *Why isn't every business run this way?*" (emphasis added)

SRC's fundamental difference is a philosophy that puts people first and communicates to a degree almost unheard of in American business. This is truly an open book company; a company that decided the hazards of not sharing information were far greater than the potential hazard of having information wind up in the wrong hands.

The first step was to teach people how to play the game. All employees went through a series of business courses: production scheduling, purchasing, accounting, plant audit, standard cost, industrial engineering, inspection and warehousing. They use the financial information system as a way to keep people focused on the effort it takes to succeed.

SRC's training program and continuous discussion of financial information has created an amazingly high level of sophistication. Shop floor personnel routinely discuss labor utilization rates, inventory turn-over, and equity ratios. At one turning point, SRC needed to build a new facility but to do that required the elimination of bonuses for one period. The employees voted to build the facility. SRC respected the employees enough to give them the responsibility for making a complex decision that required sacrificing a short-term benefit for a longer-term payoff. And the employees had the information they needed to make the best decision for the long-term well-being of the company and their investment.

Stack's confidence in and respect for the people at SRC is reflected in a statement he makes in his book, *The Great Game of Business*, "I don't disagree that machines can make you more competitive. They can absorb overhead. They don't take breaks. They don't go on vacation. They don't sit around wasting time. *What machines can't do is figure out how to make money. Only people can do that.* If you have people who know how to make money, you'll win every time. When people come to work at SRC, we tell them that 70 percent of the job is disassembly or whatever, and 30 percent of the job is learning."

The communication workhorse for SRC is the weekly

financial meeting. The process of generating and distributing financial information every week, seeing the good news and the bad news, creates an environment of trust. In addition to those meetings, SRC communicates through letters, message boards, managers who "wander around," the social environment, and daily chatter.

SRC is a transformation organization. On its way to extinction, with both feet firmly on banana peels, it found the one way to succeed. It transformed itself from a turned-off group of wage earners waiting for the ax to fall to a team of winners building equity for themselves. It happened by developing each individual in the organization . . . providing an environment that encouraged growth and ownership. The workers at SRC more than proved Stack's comment: *When you appeal to the highest level of thinking, you get the highest level of performance.* By providing all employees with a high level of information and opportunities for continued development, SRC created a growth environment. The result was an extremely committed, productive workforce and extraordinary growth and prosperity for the company.

❖
High-level thinking yields high-level performance.

Think of a specific occasion when you experienced the hazards of the myth: **What they don't know won't hurt them?** *What do you think keeps management locked into that mindset?*

The High Communication Environment

A fundamental of the transformation organization is that it communicates . . . all the time, at every level, in great detail, almost ad nauseam. Dozens of organizations such as Federal Express and Wal-Mart have discovered the value of simply letting people know how they're doing. Posting daily "critical" figures such as sales, deliveries, occupancy, time-sold, passengers, new clients or whatever, helps employees recognize their connection to the performance of the overall company.

❖
You can't communicate too much!

Organizations committed to communication encourage communication at all levels. Not only does the organization communicate information to the employees, it sets up mechanisms to stimulate the information flow from employees to the organization and the sharing of information among employees throughout the organization. E-mail, voice mail, bulletin boards, closed circuit television, meeting rooms, Friday afternoon beer busts, interdepartmental luncheons, video conferencing, newsletters. Every conceivable method of linking people is used to promote the flow of information, democratically and participatively. This doesn't mean that every communication goes to every member of the organization but it does mean that every member of the organization can communicate with any other member. When the boss is on e-mail, it's easy for the lowliest staff member to voice a complaint or offer a suggestion.

At SRC, one of the most popular channels of communication is Joann's Expressway Lounge where assembly-line workers through senior management gather after work to unwind, discuss the day and socialize. As one assembly worker says, "The barriers between management and employees just don't exist here." High communication environments find ways to continually remove the barriers between management and workers . . . barriers that destroy respect, trust and commitment if left in place.

The Communication Spectrum

The early days of radio enchanted us. Americans were glued to Roosevelt's fireside chats and entertained by "Mystery Theater" and "Amos and Andy." When television added pictures to sound, we were amazed by the antics of Lucy and Desi even when the picture was black and white and fuzzy. Color television revealed Lucy's red hair and gave us a living color window to other lands and even other galaxies. Now, interactive video begins to offer us a way to participate in the journey and virtual reality surrounds us with an image so real that it virtually seems like reality.

There is a natural progression in this trail of technology that provides us with clues to developing a high communication environment. Each level of the spectrum involves more of our senses, for instance:

Radio:	Sound only
Television:	Sound plus images
Color TV:	Sound plus color images
Interactive Video:	Sound, color images, plus user participation
Virtual Reality:	All the above plus kinesthetic stimulation and an environment that surrounds the user

Each leap in technology extends the medium to more of our senses and increases the impact of the message. Communication methods also vary in their impact. Announcements made over a public address system engage only the auditory sense of the listeners while face-to-face meetings can involve all the senses . . . if there's coffee and donuts available. The more senses involved in the communication process, the higher the impact of the communication and the more it will be remembered. Here's a breakdown of the standard types of communication by the senses they involve:

Audio only:	Announcements, speeches with no visual aids, voice mail
Visual only:	Memos, e-mail, bulletin boards, newsletters, reports
Audio & visual:	Speeches with visual aids, meeting presentations, videos, closed circuit television
Multi-Sensory & Participative:	Meetings, video conferencing, co-active communication

The lowest impact communication involves only one sense (audio or visual). To add impact, increase the sensory involvement of the communication.

Co-Active Communication

When people want to think together, resolve problems together, and create together, their communications must have impact, be quickly comprehended, maintain a big picture overview of the process and stimulate involvement. The communication should be "co-active." Co-active communication has the following qualities:

❖
Co-active:
Effective exchange
of ideas and
information

Multi-Sensory — information is presented in a way that it can be heard, seen and touched.

Open — all members of the process may participate freely without regard to status or seniority. Ideas are freely contributed and not "owned."

❖

See the forest
and the trees.

Inclusive — active participation and sharing of ideas among all members is a goal. Ideas and suggestions are actively supported and encouraged; judgment is delayed.

Co-active communication processes create an information-rich environment which supports growth, increases creativity, builds team cohesion, speeds the flow of information, identifies gaps in information or processes, and improves comprehension. Co-active communication facilitates "big picture" thinking as well as keeping a wealth of details in view and useable. Section III will provide you with several thinking tools that are based on co-active communication processes.

What's Your Organization's TQ (Transformation Quotient)?

The following evaluation will help you determine how ready your organization is for transformation. Rate your organization from 1 to 5 on the following questions.

        1 = terrible/never
        2 = poor/seldom
        3 = average/generally
        4 = good/often
        5 = excellent/always

_____ 1. We stimulate communication by providing conference rooms, whiteboards, bulletin boards, open work areas.

_____ 2. We share information widely through group meetings, newsletters, e-mail, closed circuit TV, financial and performance reports.

_____ 3. We have a high level of trust and respect for each other.

_____ 4. Meaningful training and learning opportunities are available for all members of our organization.

_____ 5. We encourage people to work together on projects and allow them to identify potential projects even when it takes time away from "normal" duties.

_____ 6. Our vision and objectives are clearly understood by all members of our organization.

____ 7. Rewards and risks are shared equitably by everyone in the organization.

____ 8. We celebrate our heroes and successes loudly and frequently.

____ 9. We have open access to everyone in the organization.

____10. Most of the time, most of our people feel pride in their work and frequently talk about work being "fun."

_____ **Total Score**

50 Perfect!   **Congratulations!** Check your perceptions with the first 5 people you meet. If they rate these questions the same way you do, call us . . . we would like to hear your story!

45-49   Yours is a rare organization. Somehow you've managed to do what everyone else is talking about doing. Keep up the good work!

40-44   You're on the right track but you need to open your lines of communications. Ask people (all people) what would make their work life better? What tools do they need? What information do they need? Do they understand the work processes and how they fit into the whole?

39 or less   Organize some transformation groups to discuss problems . . . before it's too late. There's a crack in your organization that could lead to major problems.

22 Clues to the Transformation Environment

Rubbermaid averaged a new product introduction *every day* in 1992. In an economy that saw 97,000 business failures, companies are required to find new ways to continue growing. Rubbermaid decided to develop new products faster than the competition. To facilitate the development of ideas for new products, they held a two-day internal product fair that included people from all divisions. The company estimates that over 2,000 new ideas were produced in the two days of cross-pollination.

❖
2,000 ideas
in 2 days!

Rubbermaid's former CEO Walter Williams stated: *We're a new-product-machine. We absolutely refuse not to grow.*

When you walk into an organization that has successfully achieved or is on its way to transformation, the difference in the environment is immediately apparent. While each organization has its own personality and culture, look for the following clues:

- ❐ white boards and easel pads in meeting rooms, common areas, and offices

- ❐ lots of open-access bulletin boards

- ❐ walls covered with charts, graphs, flowcharts, and project maps

- ❐ pictures of employees doing things together both at work and socially

- ❐ product demonstrations or product pictures on display

- ❐ pictures of customers using products or special boards for customer comments, survey results or letters

- ❐ frequent clustering of people working on problems, issues and ideas

- ❐ open doors throughout the organization

- ❐ high energy cafeterias used by all levels and often subsidized

- ❐ high contribution to community and charitable organizations — United Way, adopt-a-school, matching funds, etc.

- ❐ high level of involvement in sports and social activities

- ❐ first-come, first-serve parking

- ❐ absence of executive perks — "mahogany row," executive dining rooms, etc.

- ❐ employee-oriented newsletters — employee stories, celebration of personal events, reports on social activities, pictures

- ❑ shared information — sales, profits, shipments or other financial goals posted for all to see

- ❑ personalized workspaces, sometimes radically personalized

- ❑ frequent celebrations at the organization, department and individual level — from birthday parties to award presentations

- ❑ frequent training opportunities open to all

- ❑ frequent sighting of company t-shirts, hats and other insignia

- ❑ company legends — stories of success or outlandish events or deals

- ❑ high level of acceptance of diversity and tolerance of eccentricity

- ❑ last but definitely not least: lots of laughter!

Look around you — which transformation environment clues do you see? What could you do to make your environment more "transformation friendly?"

The clues listed above are not just cosmetics or window dressings that management can dictate or manipulate. They are the underlying clues that the organization supports individual growth and transformation. One of the saddest organizations we have come across to date is a civilian repair facility for military planes. An organization once known for its quality work has degenerated over the years until it looks like something out of a 1950s organizational horror story. The facility is an OSHA nightmare and one of the most frequent complaints is about the lack of basic tools (wrenches, screw drivers, etc.) to do the job. But, you don't even have to talk to the people to suspect there is a problem. The first clue hangs on a wall three feet inside the door. It's a nice wooden display case with glass doors. At the top of the case a brass plaque reads: "Artisan of the month." *The case is empty.*

On the other hand, look at Branch Banking & Trust Company (BB&T) where people even wear BB&T socks. Headquartered in Wilson, North Carolina, BB&T is the oldest bank in the state. Ten years ago, BB&T began a transformation process that resulted in extraordinary growth in a time when other financial institutions were struggling and failures were common. Although BB&T is far from the largest bank in the country, it was recently rated one of the top ten stocks by the *Wall Street Journal*'s "Smart Money" and was voted the number one bank in the country by a leading industry magazine.

BB&T is a great place to work — it provides exceptional training and growth opportunities, shares profits, contributes generously to community causes and regularly celebrates success. BB&T turnover statistics are far lower than the banking industry but sometimes stories tell more about the "feel" of an organization than numbers. Russell Thompson, director of public relations, describes the BB&T pin that employees wear. "It's an attractive pin with gold BB&T letters. Everybody wears them and we all say it helps us cash checks around town. One day someone forgot to wear his pin and everyone kidded him saying he'd left it on his pajamas!"

BB&T first came to our attention when a consultant told us about meeting a BB&T employee in the grocery store on a Saturday morning. The consultant mentioned the person's BB&T t-shirt and BB&T hat. The woman grinned, pulled up her pant leg and said, *"I'm even wearing BB&T socks!"*

In *Productive Workplaces*, Marvin Weisbord gives an excellent summation of the importance of creating a growth environment:

❖

Quantum leap
values

> *As work becomes more complicated and uncertain, I believe the values of dignity, meaning, and community will increasingly serve democratic societies as anchor points, bedrock concepts underlying quantum leaps in output, product quality and the quality of life itself.*

Creating a growth environment requires transformation thinking. Organizations cannot be transformed until they change their thinking and improve the thinking skills of every member of the organization. Transformation thinking is about identifying and achieving an organization's vision by using the power thinking skills of every member of the organization. Organizations that have mastered transformation thinking show the following qualities:

❏   high levels of group morale, individual growth, and rapid progress toward the organization's goals

❏   an unusual degree of commitment to the group goals

❏   extraordinary levels of communication between individuals and the organization

❏   shared ownership of results and rewards

❏   frequent celebrations and individual or group recognitions

❏   an environment of respect and trust for every member of the organization.

Every day we hear more and more about the Information Age, change and chaos . . . what we need now is specific guidance about how to cope with it. The next section provides practical ideas about how to flourish in the rising tide of information that threatens to engulf us.

Chapter Mindmap

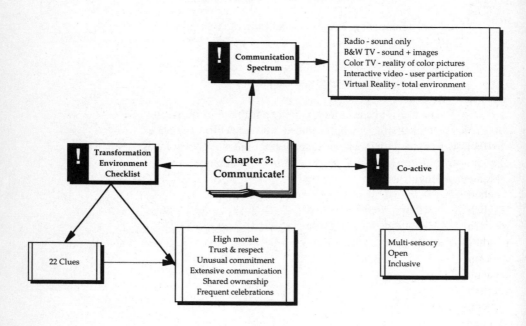

TRANSFORMATION THINKING

Everyone is born a genius.
Society degeniuses them.
— Buckminster Fuller, Inventor-Philosopher

Sometimes a Shining Moment

In Rabun Gap, Georgia, in 1966, a young high school teacher was having trouble stimulating his students' interest in English. They didn't see the connection to their lives and told the new teacher that they were going to hate the subject no matter who taught it. It was Eliot Wigginton's first teaching assignment and he took on the challenge of finding a way to interest them. He started by asking the students to write about their experiences and views of English. The responses reflected frustration and failure. One student wrote, "To read out loud is like ordering a big fat F." Small wonder the students weren't interested in a subject that was so closely connected with failure.

Wigginton tried many different approaches but each one met with little success. Finally on a bleak fall day, Wigginton walked into his first period class, sat down on top of his desk, crossed his legs, and said, "Look, this isn't working. You know it isn't and I know it isn't. Now what are we going to do together to make it through the rest of this year?" That admission opened an honest discussion about English, school, and learning. The students talked and Wigginton listened and the unlikely result was that the students decided they wanted to publish their own magazine. There were a few obstacles, however, including the fact that no one in the school or community thought the students capable of such a project. There was zero money, equipment, or staff support available, and no one really knew how to produce a magazine. (Wigginton had worked briefly on a student magazine.)

But enthusiasm for the project grew as the students generated ideas for the contents of the magazine: their own stories, poems and art work as well as that of students from other schools, and creative work by professional writers and artists. They also decided to include feature articles about the surrounding community, initially as a way to encourage sales. As the vision began to come together, students from all six of Wigginton's classes brainstormed titles and finally settled on *Foxfire* — the name of a fungus that grows on decaying organic matter in damp, dark coves in the mountains and glows in the dark.

The students interviewed their elders in the rural, mountain area; wrote articles, stories and poems; sold subscriptions; took photographs; and finally produced 600 copies of their first magazine. A second printing sold out almost as fast as the first. The first issue of *Foxfire* was passed across the country and recognition began to pour in. More subscriptions were sold and the next issue was planned; soon *Foxfire* became a popular quarterly magazine. One copy wound up in the hands of an editor from Doubleday who thought it would make an interesting book.

He was right. Over two million copies of the first *The Foxfire Book* have been sold and *Foxfire 10* was released in April, 1993, making the *Foxfire* series Doubleday's best selling series. Wigginton and his students kicked off a wave of cultural journalism and, through their efforts, preserved the cultural heritage of their North Georgia mountain area.

The Learning Organization

The literary efforts of Wigginton and his students are impressive but, on a larger scale, the Foxfire methods may change the fundamental approach to education and offer clues to the development of a learning organization. Money from the *Foxfire* series was used to start The Foxfire Fund, Inc., a non-profit educational organization. In the mid-1980s, the Fund received a major grant to be used to determine if the teaching methods which had proven so successful in rural Georgia would also work in other environments with other teachers and other school facilities.

The practices proved transferrable and today there is a growing network of teachers nationwide who study and refine the Foxfire approach. They have developed a set of core practices focusing on the students as active participants in their own learning process.

The following stories from a recent meeting of the Foxfire Teacher Outreach are just a sample of the types of activities occurring in classrooms across the country:

II

> **First Grade Play:** A first grade class in Washington asked the question, "Could dinosaurs ever have lived here in Silver Lake?" Because their teacher didn't have the answer, the students decided to find out themselves. They began to read books, watch films and have their parents read books to them. They invited a paleontologist from the University of Washington to come to their class so they could interview him. They even did a fake archeological dig on the playground.
>
> Once they had done their research, they decided to write a three act play (based on the three periods when dinosaurs had lived) including two songs and a choreographed dance. (They answered their original question in the second song.) The kids talked their parents into sewing costumes to their specifications (they had to be fabric), wrote the play, rehearsed and presented it to a group of parents and neighbors (they had designed their own flyers and posted them throughout the neighborhood).
>
> After the performance, they decided it wasn't good enough, so they revised the play and then presented it again to the entire school.
>
> **Middle School Community Project:** In a middle school a stone's throw away from Disney World in Florida, Lee Powell was given the Dropout Prevention Program. She quickly realized that in order to turn the kids on to school, she was going to have to find a way to turn them on to life. She discovered that the kids wanted action . . . they wanted to do something. Together, they discovered an old cannery barn in the community that had fallen into a state of disrepair and decided to renovate it for use as a community center. They negotiated a $1 per year lease

II

and began the renovation process. As the work started, some of the senior citizens from the area began to come around and talk to the students, demonstrate their crafts, and help with the renovation work. It gradually became a place for inter-generational "hanging out."

High School Play: A high school writing class decided to write a play about the problems facing high school students. They worked out all the details and logistics together and after the play had been written and revised several times, they decided to actually present the play and do the acting themselves. They rehearsed for a month and a half, constantly rewriting and revising as they went. Finally they presented the play for three nights to the school. The process of acting out the play changed their perceptions so much that they continued to revise and rewrite the play for three weeks after school was out.

Interesting things happen when people are actively involved in their own projects. The first graders in Silver Lake, Washington, who were writing the play about dinosaurs developed a snag along the way. It was two days before the performance and the song committee still didn't have one. One of the children approached the teacher and told her they couldn't come up with a song . . . she would have to. The teacher told them that it was ok with her if they didn't have a song but if they wanted one they would have to do it themselves. The student sighed and said, "I knew you would say that!" She returned to her committee and by the next day they had a song and a choreographed dance.

Foxfire has proven that ordinary classrooms can be transformed into dynamic learning environments. A similar transformation can occur in any organization when every member of the organization becomes an important, participating part of the whole . . . when each member is taught fundamental but powerful thinking skills and the dynamics of how to think together.

The next three chapters focus on the thinking processes necessary for transformation. Chapter 4 gives you an overview of how the two parts of our minds work together. Chapter 5 provides specific guidance for getting groups of people thinking together and Chapter 6 shows you how to avoid eight common thinking pitfalls.

Transformation Thinking

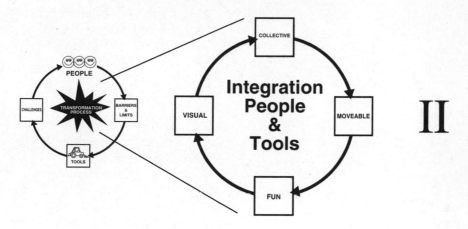

II

COMING ATTRACTIONS

"Jud"   "Gen"

three stages

divergence
stimulators

consensus
stimulators

TWO THINKERS

TWO
THINKERS

To know what you do not know,
You must go where you have not gone,
See what you have not seen,
Do what you have not done,
And be what you have not been.

Two worlds exist in separate spaces, as different as night and day, touching only at their outer edges. The world of day is bright with streets laid out straight and well-marked. The world of night is murky with paths twisting and turning and sometimes abruptly stopping or dropping off into a different space.

Most of us have become day people. We like knowing where we are and seeing the path lying straight before us. The night place frightens us; we might lose our way or fall into the unknown. To prevent our falling into that dark abyss, we put up barriers around our day space. Because of our fear, we've locked ourselves away from half of our world.

We've lost the cool, dark, alluring richness of the night-space. Gradually we forgot that we were born to explore the night as well as the day and that we had candles to guide our way through the darkness. As we stayed more and more in the world of the day, the dark-place became more of a mystery . . . some even said a fantasy. Occasional travelers to the night-land were scoffed at and any night-place treasures had to be smuggled into the day-land.

But the lure of the night-land was powerful, and courageous travelers continued to explore its spaces. When a great chaos threatened the day-world, intrepid travelers told of a great wealth that existed in the night-world which could cure the troubles. But to retrieve the bounty, the day-world barriers would need to be dropped and all people would have to journey into the night-world to carry back their portion of the treasure.

And, that's where we are today . . . in the midst of a great chaos . . . trying to run our world and solve our problems with only part of our resources. Split-brain studies in the sixties identified two very different sets of traits that were handled by the separate brain hemispheres. Further research showed that one set of traits — the logical, analytical skills of the "left-brain" (our day-world) — were being emphasized far more than the visual, pattern-making, intuitive skills of the "right-brain" (our night-world).

Subsequent studies have revealed much more cross-over in which traits are handled on each side of the brain, however, the terms "right-brain/left-brain" are still a useful way to refer to certain sets of traits which we each possess but use to a greater or lesser degree. We can think of these sets of traits as two "thinkers" residing in our brain.

The Whole-Brain Team

These two thinkers make up the team we need for whole-brain thinking. Here's a description of each thinker's strengths and short-comings:

> **The Judge ("Jud")** likes things neat and organized and puts emphasis on what's important today or what worked yesterday. "Jud" is logical, practical and uses words to communicate thoughts, ideas and commands. "Jud" adds things up to come to a conclusion and breaks something down into its parts in order to analyze it, believing in first things first and making sure each step is right.

> **The Generator ("Gen")** likes to think about possibilities and the future. "Gen" is stimulated by images and color and needs to see the whole picture. "Gen" skips around making connections that have never been made before, putting things together that seemingly have no business being together (waffles on shoes — Nike; burrs on socks — velcro; a boy on a light beam — Einstein's theory of

relativity) and not worrying for a second about
practicality.

"Jud" and "Gen" make a great team . . . except for one
problem. "Jud" is verbal and extremely good at communicating . . .
"Gen" is mute and communicates only with pictures and feelings.
After years of emphasizing verbal skills in school and
organizational life, "Jud" became much stronger than "Gen" and
eventually started to believe that "Gen" wasn't all that smart or
important. "Gen" began to fade into the background, refusing to
come out if "Jud" was around, and took on the role of a playmate,
someone to do hobbies or other, less important activities with. The
conflict between them left us using half our brain to solve
problems and make decisions . . . we were stuck in the day-world.

Creativity, innovation, and critical thinking require both
thinkers — "Gen" gives us possibilities and shows us new ways to
do things; "Jud" helps us make those new ideas useful and plan
their implementation. But to have them both working for us, we
have to let "Gen" come out for awhile before we let "Jud" in the
room. When "Jud" walks in with a judgmental, take-charge
attitude, "Gen" skips away into the darkness and stubbornly
ignores all our coaxing to return.

Ralph Waldo Emerson said: *In every work of genius, we
recognize our own rejected thoughts: they come back to us with a
certain alienated majesty.* The ideas we reject as too stupid or silly
to mention may wind up being tomorrow's brilliance. In 1927,
Harry Warner of the legendary Warner Brothers film studio said:
Who the hell wants to hear actors talk? Marva Collins, the much-
heralded teacher from Chicago says: *You must believe in your own
thoughts, because if you don't, somebody else will say what you
were afraid to say.*

Three Stages of Thinking

Almost everyone knows we need more creativity and
innovation, yet we still try to "spreadsheet" our way out of our
problems. We tend to jump at the first right answer and insist on
logic at every step. Countless surveys of executives indicate that
creativity, innovation and critical thinking are among their top
concerns and yet there's only a handful of companies that conduct
any kind of organized thinking training. Ask any CEO how
important thinking is and the answer will almost always come

back, "Extremely." Then ask how many training classes are devoted to thinking skills. Notice the long pause. There is a definite discontinuity in what we say and what we do.

Perhaps it's the terminology. Maybe "left- and right-brain" is too mysterious for us. It could be that "creativity" sounds too nebulous. Or innovation seems like something they do in engineering . . . or at Disneyland. So, let's look at it differently; let's think about the basic thinking processes, consisting of:

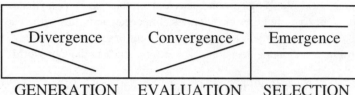

| Divergence | Convergence | Emergence |

GENERATION   EVALUATION   SELECTION

❐   idea generation — emphasis: divergence

❐   idea evaluation — emphasis: convergence

❐   idea selection — emphasis: emergence

These three thinking processes exist whether we're trying to solve a problem, develop an agenda for a meeting, come up with new product ideas, improve a process, or decide what to have for lunch.

The important thing to remember about these elements is:

They cannot exist at the same time!

The minute you begin to evaluate, creation is over. And, selection ends the evaluation process. In our day-world, we have become experts at evaluation and selection. Our school system taught us evaluation and selection skills and our organization life faithfully rewards the people who excel in these abilities. The more successful we've been in an organization, the more likely that we are highly skilled evaluators and selectors.

Edward de Bono, one of our foremost "thinking" gurus (author of about 30 books on the thinking process) who has a term for almost everything, calls this phenomenon "Catch 24." Catch 24 states:

*In order to reach the senior position in an organization,
you should be without, or have kept hidden, **exactly those
talents you will need when you get there.***

De Bono is talking about idea generation — about that
spark that allows you to see new vistas, do the "vision thing," and
lead others to catch the same vision. In most organizations, this
talent, applied too early, is the kiss of death, the mark of the misfit,
the troublemaker, the non-team player . . . and the sure route to a
dark corner in the basement or a termination for "mutual reasons."

❖
Idea generation is
messy, uncertain
and uncontrollable.

Idea generation requires a journey into the night-land, a
connection with the messy, non-straight-forward, generative parts
of our minds. This walk on the dark side creates many problems
for us. Here are just a few:

❐ **Tension.** Problems create a tension which demands to be
eased immediately. Therefore, we seize on the first
possible answer in order to solve the problem and ease the
tension. Generating lots of possibilities would mean
prolonging the tension and thus possibly increasing our
anxiety.

❐ **Speed.** We're into speed. We want answers . . . and
solutions . . . right now. If we spend time brainstorming
possible ideas, then it's going to take just that much
longer to find an answer. We want to get on with it and
solve the problem now . . . today . . . this minute!

❐ **Efficiency.** Most of the stuff we come up with in a
brainstorming session isn't really useful so we might as
well just use logic and get to the right answer
immediately. However, this approach means that we limit
our choices and too often take the first answer as the only
answer.

❐ **One right answer.** We're used to thinking that there is
one right answer so if we find an answer that's right . . . it
must be the right answer! The concept of many right
answers is foreign to us.

❐ **Harmony.** We have a cultural bias towards politeness and
agreement or maybe it's just a fear of disagreement,
perhaps going back to the days when disagreements were

settled with a Colt 45. Generating lots of possibilities usually involves getting a multitude of ideas and opinions bouncing around all at once in an atmosphere that resembles chaos more than harmony.

The idea generation stage is time consuming, messy and often loud and heated. It's also effective. If you can afford to operate with half your resources, you can afford to avoid this stage. If you can't, you need to learn how to use it.

What's your organization's mindset about thinking? Does it honor all three thinking processes? Which process is the weakest?

Divergence

In the idea generation stage of thinking, you have to have divergence. You have to generate lots of different ideas. People have to be encouraged to disagree with each other or to hear one idea and say the opposite even if it sounds stupid. They have to understand that they will not be held responsible for what they say during this stage. They can say orange is purple and it will be non-judgmentally recorded. No one cares because at this divergent stage, the goal is to create a large quantity of ideas that can be sifted, sorted, tweaked, bent or thrown away completely in the next stage. (Besides maybe there's some value in purple oranges.)

Think about Henry Ford when he said customers could have any color car they wanted ... as long as it was black. Imagine Henry sitting alone going through the thinking process:

Idea generation stage:	Possible colors for car . . . hmm . . . black.
Idea evaluation stage:	I like black.
Idea selection stage:	Black it is.

You have to admit, with only one possibility, the process is simple and clean. But then Henry didn't have a lot of competition to worry about and he didn't have that nagging problem of customer service and customer complaints. People back then were still stunned at the idea of a motorized vehicle so color and "niceties" weren't important.

But, for today's organizations, the honeymoon period gets shorter all the time and few have the luxury of one-choice decisions. Competition forces us to constantly generate new ideas, new products, new ways to deliver products to customers, new packaging, new services, new pricing schemes, new colors, new shapes, new smells, new sounds, new tastes, and new ways to tell people about all the new stuff.

Cream Rises . . . Creativity Lurks on Bottom

Fresh-from-the-cow, unpasteurized, non-homogenized, non-vitamin-fortified milk, when allowed to sit, forms a layer of cream on top. This used to be called the "good stuff" back in our old, pre-fat-conscious days. Creative ideas are the opposite of cream . . . they don't rise to the top of our minds; they lurk on bottom waiting to be stirred up.

The ideas that rise to the top of our minds are cliches, the ideas that we've thought before, the platitudes spoken by other people, the bromides, the stereotypes and the comfortable, commonplace, old tunes we've heard a million times. Therefore, when we take the first possibility that pops into our head as the answer to a problem, we are probably getting old thinking. The idea may sound good because it's familiar . . . and it might be a good idea. But it isn't the only idea or even the only good idea. The only way to get to the good ideas is to stir up your thinking . . . wake up some of that creativity lurking at the bottom and get it circulating.

Research shows that the most innovative, novel, fresh solutions tend to be found among the last half of the ideas generated on any topic. It is critical to stimulate divergent thinking in order to get to this pool of fresh, creative ideas.

❖
The best ideas come last.

Idea Stimulators

Here are just a few of the many ways to stimulate divergence (many of these processes will be discussed in more detail in the following chapters):

❏ **brainstorm** — Generate as many ideas as possible in a fixed period of time — no judgments, wild ideas encouraged. Chapter 7 will show you how to make your brainstorming sessions more productive.

❐ **perfect world** — Think about what it would look like if you had the perfect solution to your problem or situation. In a perfect world what would your product/service/idea look like? In a perfect world, cars would never break down, never get dirty, never need gas or oil, never go out of style, etc. In a perfect world, the customer would never be unhappy, never have to return a product, never have to pay for the product, never have to make an effort to get the product, etc. Look at each "perfect" criteria and generate ideas about how to achieve it or use it.

One of the benefits of Perfect World is the consensus that is generated when people leap over the quagmire of the current problems and realities and think about the future. Very often different factions have a great deal of agreement about the ideal result but vary enormously in their ideas about how to get there. Also looking at the possibilities generates excitement and enthusiasm which can often carry people past their individual differences. Tim recently facilitated a session for a Beach United Methodist Church group which was trying to decide how to improve attendance for their family night program. In less than an hour they generated over 60 ideas and then used dot voting to select the ideas they wanted to implement. The shocking part of the process was that when they presented the plan to the Council on Ministeries, a group that had previously expressed extreme reservations about changing the program, it was adopted unanimously.

Perfect World is an excellent planning tool. A group can visualize what the perfect situation would be in five years and then work backwards from that point, identifying where they would need to be at the end of each year.

❐ **set quotas** — Generate at least 5 (or 10 or 100) ideas before considering any of them.

❐ **opposites** — Automatically suggest the opposite when an idea is generated. Dawn Steel in her book *They Can Kill You . . . But They Can't Eat You, Lessons from the Front* tells a story that demonstrates the power of opposites. She and her husband were in Miami when they saw a woman wearing everything Gucci — Gucci scarf, shoes, handbag, bracelet, earrings, watch, blouse, everything. They looked at each other and asked, "Is there anything in the world that doesn't have those G's on it?" The immediate answer was "toilet paper!" They created the first "designer toilet paper" — a Gucci knock-off— which became the hot fad item of the season. A few minutes of "opposite" thinking yielded a blockbuster idea.

❐ **bouncing** — Take any idea and bounce around on it, saying whatever words come to mind.

❐ **forced comparison** — Pick any object and think through your idea using the qualities of that item. If you're trying to improve customer service, think of the qualities of an apple (round, red, sweet, smooth, living, nourishing, eye appealing, colorful, cool, firm) and think about those qualities in relationship to your customer service.

❐ **"what if"** — Play "what if" to imagine the most unusual possibilities — what if cars didn't have to be painted, what if leaves didn't have to be raked, what if children didn't have to go to school to learn, what if tires never wore out, what if computers could cook meals. Come up with 10 "what ifs" about your situation.

❐ **ask "Why?"** — Ask "Why?" about everything — why do we package our product in a box? Why do we use this color? Why that shape? Why this material? Keep going deeper and deeper with your whys. Let each answer stimulate the next why.

❐ **how else** — How else could this be done? What other ways are there to accomplish this objective?

❐ **different chair** — Assume someone else's perspective. What does the situation look like to the customer . . . to a different department . . . to a newcomer . . . to a child . . . to an old person or a handicapped person?

❐ **stupid and ridiculous** — Generate 5 or 10 really stupid ideas. Have the group be as far out as possible then look at the ideas to see if they have any value or could be the basis for other ideas.

Richard Hadden, a Jacksonville, Florida, trainer/
consultant, was not satisfied with his marketing efforts.
He was making lots of calls every day but his results
weren't keeping up with his efforts. He and Tim sat down
to discuss possible ways to improve his efforts and
decided to use *Stupid & Ridiculous* to generate non-
traditional ideas. One of the ideas thrown out was to let
his 5-year old daughter do his marketing. Bouncing on
that idea led them to thinking about addressing envelopes
with crayons and that led to the idea of having a mailing
piece with two "faces" — one "face" would appeal to the
child-like, playful, right-brain and the other "face" would
appeal to the business-like, results-oriented left-brain.
The marketing piece is still in development so we don't
know what the final results will be but two things are
certain: Richard has developed a marketing piece that will
differentiate him from other trainer/consultants and he
has broken his traditional thought barriers regarding his
marketing efforts.

There's nothing magic about these idea stimulators. They
don't automatically create brilliant ideas; they just shake things up
and get ideas moving. Remember the snow globes we had as
children? If you turned them upside down, the snow would swirl
around the winter scene inside the globe. These stimulators are
like turning the globe upside down to make it snow. Ideas begin to
float around and bounce into each other. New combinations
happen and we have more ideas to choose from when we go into
the idea evaluation stage.

*Think of a situation where one or more of these idea
stimulators would be useful. Try it!*

Caution: Be Prepared for the Fire Hydrant Syndrome

If you decide to use one or more of these stimulators, it's
important to know how to deal with the overwhelming quantity of
ideas you may generate. (Some folks say it's like trying to drink
from a fire hydrant!) The most important thing you need to do is
capture the ideas on paper. Confucious reportedly said: *Short
pencil better than long memory.* Not a bad philosophy even if he
really didn't say it. Make sure all of your meetings and thinking
sessions have someone designated as a idea recorder.

You can use some of the convergence stimulators given below to organize and synthesize the ideas into useful action plans.

Convergence . . . Emergence

Once we've generated a lot of ideas, we begin to evaluate, adapt and discard. We winnow the wheat from the chaff and decide which ideas would work in our situation. In group thinking processes, there is often a resistance to convergence because of "turf" issues. Here are some ways to stimulate convergence:

- ❏ **Dot Voting** — give each person three to five colored dot "votes" which can be cast for the ideas the person thinks most important — one dot for each choice or all the votes for one if the person thinks it is that important.

- ❏ **Weighting** — have each person rank each suggestion from 1 to 5 (1 for least important and 5 for most important) and narrow the field to the top weighted ideas.

- ❏ **Pairings** — once the field is narrowed to less than 20, pair each choice to see which is more important. There is computer voting technology available which takes most of the drudgery out of this process. (See Chapter 9 for a discussion of CoNexus, a technology that handles pairings.)

Once certain ideas begin to rise from the pack, they can be subjected to closer scrutiny, data gathering and analysis, and trial runs. Gradually, a solution begins to emerge and the participative decision-making process brings the group together to support the chosen path.

What's your organization's primary barrier to achieving agreement on ideas and action plans? Generate five ideas for breaking through that barrier . . . then generate three stupid and ridiculous ones.

The New Critical Thinking

The new critical thinking is more than a concern for logic and facts. It blends the skills of left-brain analysis with the right-brain ability to recognize patterns and trends. This whole-brain style of thinking has the ability to shift focus and look at ideas, information and problems from new perspective. Ray Payn, a multi-media software developer and student of thinking processes, provided us with the following list of examples of critical thinking shifts:

TWO THINKERS

Shift from:	To:
Looking at what's there	Looking for what's not there
Seeking conclusions	Checking assumptions
Examining details	Evaluating concepts
Concern about the goal	Regard for the process
Today's problems	Tomorrow's challenges
Focus on objects	Importance of relationships
Contents	Container
Tense concentration	Relaxed flow
Object	Surrounding space
What is said	What is unsaid

Understanding how to get both halves of our brain working together is a critical part of improving our thinking process. The next step is getting several minds working together . . . at the same time. The following chapter will explain how to get groups of people thinking together effectively.

Chapter Mindmap

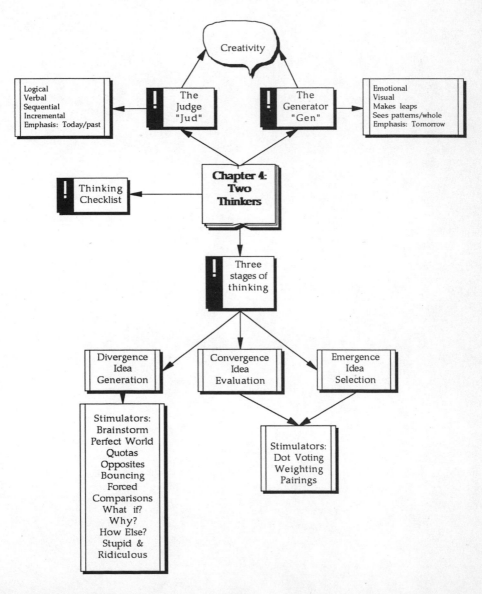

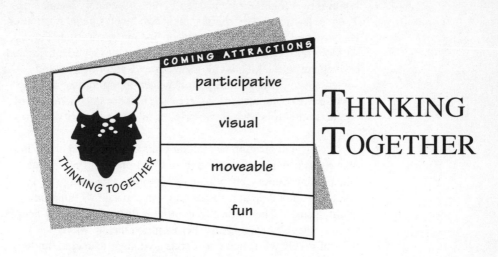

CHAPTER 5

THINKING TOGETHER

- participative
- visual
- moveable
- fun

Only a group of people who share a body of knowledge and continually learn together can stay vital and viable.
— Max DePree, Chairman of Herman Miller, Inc. and author of **The Art of Management**

When Motorola discovered a revolutionary video screen produced by a small company in Oregon, the giant company moved with the speed of an entrepreneur. In less than a month, Motorola's CEO met with the officers of the Oregon firm and three months later the two companies announced a joint venture to manufacture the screens in the US. A month later the product was launched.

❖ Big doesn't have to mean slow.

Motorola is one of the few US giants that has managed spectacular success in a time of chaos. Its well-known "six sigma," near-perfection, quality program has been credited with an estimated savings of $3.1 billion in the past five years. The Motorola culture spawns thousands of small teams and consistently devotes an inordinate amount of time and money to employee development. During one recent year, the price tag for teaching employees how to identify and fix problems amounted to $70 million. But, perhaps its most unusual quality is a unique environment that actually kindles conflict and dissention.

❖ Open, honest discussion weeds out weak ideas.

Dissent and open, verbal combat are the norm within the Motorola family and employees are entitled to file a minority report if they feel their ideas aren't being adequately listened to. The reports are read by management two levels up and retribution is considered "unmacho" and out-of-line in the corporate culture. At Motorola, open, often heated, discussion quickly identifies and corrects mistakes, kills weak ideas, spreads information, and sometimes unearths unlikely blockbuster opportunities. The 68000-series computer microprocessor that became the brains of Apple Computer's Macintosh originated with a minority report.

The dedication to making products better and cheaper than rivals in Japan also came from Motorola's cult of dissent when Arthur Sundry, then head of Motorola's two-way radio operations, stood up at a social function and said, "I think our quality stinks." The culture of conflict is difficult for many people. Even former CEO George Fisher admitted that he was uncomfortable with such conflict as a younger manager, but was eventually convinced that "out of conflict comes catharsis."

Motorola operates in a fast-breaking, high-tech world of innovations, price reductions and obsolescenses. The culture is designed to keep critical information flowing quickly throughout the organization. For years they have had an intelligence department whose job it was to build technology roadmaps that assess where breakthroughs are likely to occur. A *Wall Street Journal* profile stated, "Anticipation is a religion at Motorola."

❖
Motorola Magic:
Think together &
respect individual
contributions

From 1987 to 1992, Motorola's productivity doubled and after it became one of the first Malcolm Baldrige National Quality Award winners in 1988, Rosabeth Moss Kanter, former editor of the *Harvard Business Review*, stated, "Motorola is one of the few genuine role models of industry transformation." Motorola has learned to think together and to respect the contribution of each individual.

Thinking Together Is Not the Same as a Committee

Several years ago, Joyce had the opportunity to experience a management development workshop with the well-known psychologist Mason Haire. One of the exercises during the workshop was "Desert Survival," which involved the ranking of ten items in the order of their importance for survival following a plane crash in the desert. The exercise had each individual in the group rank the items then small groups were formed to develop a group consensus. One fascinating result of this exercise was that the scores of the small groups were always higher than the scores of the individuals within the group. Pooling the intelligence of the individual members of the group yielded a higher intelligence than that of any member . . . a perfect example of synergy, where the whole is greater than the sum of its parts.

Though years of organizational life had hardened a "committees don't work" mentality, seeing the dynamics of the Desert Survival exercise was a breakthrough. Obviously there was an advantage to thinking together. But what was the difference between a committee and a group of people sharing information and thinking effectively together? What was it about committees and meetings that made them so ineffective? Why did people dread going to them?

To help identify the differences between a committee and a group of people thinking effectively together, let's look at what is too often a typical meeting scenario :

THINKING TOGETHER

> It's 3:00 p.m. and ten people slowly file into a small conference room. The boss enters last and takes the seat at the head of the table. The boss talks; the others take notes. The boss asks for a report and one of the others reports. The boss comments. Next topic. The boss talks. Another report; another boss comment. The boss asks for questions; everyone shuffles papers, avoids eye contact, and waits for the magic word: adjourned.
> P.S. . . . same time next week.

What's wrong with this picture? It's not a meeting (an act or process of coming together); it's a performance . . . a sham. There's little information transferred, few ideas exchanged, no real discussion, and limited participation. Meetings like the one described above are window dressing . . . attempts to make people feel like they're a part of something without giving them any real power or involvement.

PONDER BREAK

On a scale of 1 to 10 (1 = never; 10 = always), how often does your organization display the synergy that comes from good thinking together skills?

Thinking Together Philosophies

Transformation thinking requires going beyond window dressing. It requires a mutual sharing of information, a commitment to group learning and a common objective. It requires a genuine meeting where people come together in mutual respect, honesty and trust. There are several underlying philosophies required for getting people to think together productively:

THINKING TOGETHER

❐ **Give people as many chances as possible to interact.** Make it easy for people to share ideas and information informally as well as formally. An incredible amount of "work" is done at water fountains, in rest rooms and in cafeterias. Easy-access conference rooms, round tables, white boards, easel pads, and bulletin boards make it easy to share information, work out solutions and have spur-of-the-moment brainstorming sessions.

❐ **Remove participation barriers.** The richest settings for thinking together occur when the group is varied in backgrounds, expertise, age, and points of view. However, these differences also create status barriers including rank or position, information or expertise, age or seniority, or turf or control. People on the lower end of those status barriers will often avoid participating for fear of looking uninformed or making a mistake that might adversely impact the person's standing or future.

In order to stimulate participation by junior members, it is critical to establish a safe environment for the thinking process. People must feel that their input is important and that their ideas will not be ridiculed or judged. Breaking down large groups into smaller groups of 3-4 reduces the performance fears and creates a safer environment. Allowing anonymous input also reduces the barriers to participation. More ideas for reducing these barriers will be presented in Chapter 7 — Better Brainstorming.

❐ **Give them as much information as possible.** Information is the energy that drives learning and thinking. Open up the organization's information — assume that everyone who wants to know has a need to know. Creativity requires the meeting of two pieces of information that were previously strangers to each other.

❏ **Push them to discover more.** Encourage people to make new discoveries and to generate more information. The push for new information may be even more important than finding solutions as new information automatically generates energy within the organization.

❏ **Encourage people to own the result . . . not the idea!** It doesn't matter who an idea belongs to or whether the person had the proper credentials to generate the idea. Does the idea work or can it be made to work? When everyone benefits from the results of ideas, they can own and celebrate those results rather than worrying about whose ideas got them there.

Which of the basics listed above is weakest in your organization? How could you strengthen it?

The Thinking Organization Core Practices

During the process of interviewing various organizations for this book, we discovered that even in highly successful companies, there was often little clarity about the thinking and learning process. In other words, there was little "conscious competence."

In order to pass along understanding of the process necessary for group transformation thinking, we needed to find an organization that had developed a clear understanding of the thinking and learning together process. The best we found was the Foxfire organization discussed in the overview to this section. Their entire focus is developing a process that stimulates transformation in students. Through their years of study and refinement, they have developed a set of eleven core practices which establish an environment where self-directed efforts lead to enthusiastic growth in a spirit of adventure. The magic of these practices is the way the needs and concerns of the students mesh with the learning objectives of the school system to produce spectacular results.

The Greek philosopher Plutarch said: *The mind is not a vessel to be filled but a fire to be ignited.* The participative learning practices which are now being used by teachers across the country can also be used to ignite participative learning and transformation thinking within organizations. The eleven Foxfire core practices

97

are just as valid for corporate America as they are for the education system. Here are those core practices translated into language appropriate for business organizations:

❏ **Democratic** — All work must flow from the concerns and desires of the group members. It must be infused from the beginning with group choice, design, revision, execution, reflection, and evaluation. Problems are solved by group collaboration.

❏ **Management functions as a collaborator/ facilitator** — Managers and supervisors monitor progress toward group goals, encourage the growth of each member and lead the group into new areas of understanding and competence.

❏ **Vision** — There should be a group vision that is larger than each individual vision. Each member should be able to see that the only way to achieve the larger vision is by working together. Members should also be able to see how the work of the group fits within the overall organizational vision.

❏ **Active participation** — Work is characterized by active involvement in the entire process rather than by passive processing of information or instructions. Active participation pushes people to the edge of their competence — which increases the possibilities of mistakes. Therefore, group members must be frequently reassured that mistakes are part of the learning and thinking process.

❏ **Inclusion** — Every worker is not only included in the group but is also needed. Each member shares information and responsibility with the other members of the group.

❏ **Connected** — Practical connections to other parts of the organization and to the real world need to be clear. Group members must see the interconnectedness of their actions and the effects of their work. Their work must be accepted and acted upon by the rest of the organization.

❏ **Audience** — There needs to be an audience for the group's efforts . . . celebrations and showcases. Pride and an appreciative audience affirm the importance of the work. Time after time, the Foxfire teachers found that it wasn't enough for their students to do a project; they needed to share their work with others. They wanted the work to be appreciated. While the project wasn't done specifically for an audience, it needed an audience for a sense of completion.

❑ **Completeness** — All work should give the group and individuals a sense of completeness and satisfaction. It should allow each person to use their imaginations and give them challenges which stimulates growth.

❑ **Reflection** — Some conscious, thoughtful time is needed to allow people to stand apart from their work. This evokes insights and nurtures revisions that lead to improvements. This is the part of the process people are least accustomed to doing especially in busy organizations where meeting deadlines takes precedence over improving processes.

❑ **Feedback** — Each project needs to be frequently evaluated with feedback provided to every member of the group. Feedback should provide information for continued improvement of skills and results.

❑ **Ongoing Growth** — Group members must be able to build on their skills and continue to develop competence and mastery. The end of one project should lead to the beginning of the next project. Each person should ask "Now what? How can we use these skills to continue?"

Which of these core practices is strongest in your organization? How can you build on that strength to improve your thinking environment?

Solectron: "People are much more capable than they think they are."

Solectron is an example of the successful transformation that can happen when a company adopts the participative thinking and learning environment defined by the Foxfire core practices. The San Jose-based organization, a 1991 Baldrige award winner, is an independent provider of customized integrated manufacturing services to original equipment manufacturers (OEMs) in the electronics industry. At Solectron, charts and posters are everywhere — charting critical performance indicators in every department — making information available to every employee and making each person part of the process of improvement. During the application for the Baldrige, posters explaining the Baldrige criteria were printed in four languages: English, Spanish, Vietnamese and Chinese.

Solectron executives learned that a sincere belief in the willingness of their employees to improve and extend an extra effort is just as important as posters and charts in a multilingual environment. President and Chief Operating Officer, Ko Nishimura states: *People are much more capable than they think they are, and they are willing to do more than you think they will.* Perhaps even more important than the Baldrige are the 32 quality awards Solectron has received from customers, including IBM, Sun Microsystems, and Hewlett-Packard.

In recent years, we've seen a lot of management fads come and go. But, some ideas have stayed and grown into widely accepted beliefs. The critical importance of the individuals within an organization is one of those beliefs. Strong backs and willing hands are no longer enough. Mindpower has replaced horsepower. The days are gone when management can sit and think and workers can stand and do. Transformation thinking requires the mindpower of all members of the organization. The organizations that will survive the turbulence of our fast-changing world are the ones that create an environment that encourages people to think together. Those organizations continuously strive to become thinking organizations, combining constant learning with powerful group thinking techniques to achieve perpetual improvement and quantum leaps.

Visual Thinking

Michael Michalko in his book, *Thinkertoys*, relates an observation by the German psychologist Wolfgang Kohler. A female ape who was able to use a stick as a rake to obtain food that was placed outside her cage lost that ability if the stick was placed behind her, outside her field of vision. In order for her to connect the use of the stick with the acquisition of food, they both had to be in her field of vision.

We're not apes and we can keep the stick in mind even if it's behind our backs. However, the principle of keeping things in our visual field is still important. Human studies have shown that most of us can only keep 7-9 items in our mind at one time. By putting information into a visual form, we can increase the amount of data we can work with. Unrecognized patterns begin to reveal themselves, connections become apparent, inefficiencies are brought to light and new possibilities pop out.

Thinking together requires visual presentation of information. Everyone in the group needs to see the information and ideas in order to stimulate their own thinking. As new ideas are added, they automatically trigger others. When we are working with information visually, we can draw relationships, link ideas, show the flow of processes and graphically present complex information in diagrams that can quickly be comprehended.

❖
To think together effectively, everyone needs to "see" the entire picture.

In Israel, an unusual educational project known as the Agam Project, sponsored by the Weizmann Institute of Science is teaching a unique visual-language curriculum to pre-schoolers. Ya'acov Agam, a renowned Israeli artist, devised a visual alphabet of circles, squares, horizontal lines, vertical lines, curves and colors. He believes, along with a growing number of educators, that the overemphasis on verbal education stifles thinking abilities in students.

After nine years, the project has delivered results which far surpass original expectations. The program not only helps children develop visual thinking and memory but it also appears to improve overall intelligence. Visual training helps the children observe, analyze, and synthesize; develop visual memory; respond to visual stimuli reflexively; and be visually creative. The visual activities enhance their awareness of patterns and increase concentration and attention.

But visual thinking isn't just for school children. It's a fundamental requirement for thinking organizations. When groups of people come together to solve problems or think of new ideas, they naturally gravitate to the nearest white board or easel pad to try to communicate ideas visually. Complex ideas and processes can be quickly diagrammed and people begin to see patterns, linkages and relationships. As people gain greater sophistication in handling information visually, there is an increase in the overall intelligence level of the group. Complex thinking and analysis tools that were formerly used only by highly-trained professionals begin to filter down to the lowest levels of the organization.

How does your group make information visual? What techniques could you use to build the visual thinking skills of your group?

The Thinker's Secret Weapon

One of our most important thinking tools isn't the all-important personal computer, the calculator, or even TQM's highly touted statistical process control . . . it's the Post-it™ note! Created by 3M, the Post-it™ note was originally a communication device that allowed us to make comments on letters or reports without damaging the original document. Post-it™ notes started out as a novelty item but rapidly became a necessity. Little yellow "stickies" started showing up everywhere.

But sticky notes are more than just a convenient way to make notes on documents. They actually contribute two major benefits to the thinking process:

❏ they're moveable
❏ they come in different shapes, sizes and colors to help facilitate the organization of information.

Across the country, as people began to work together to solve problems, map out projects, and create new ideas, they quickly discovered Post-it™ notes and began to use them in hundreds of different ways.

Anthony Nagle, a management consultant from Edina, Minnesota, uses Post-it™ notes in his negotiation training and consulting. Nagle uses "keynotes" — six-sided sticky notes whose shape stimulates the linking of ideas in unique ways. Nagle encourages the groups he's working with to turn the negotiation process away from face-to-face adversarial bargaining to mutual problem-solving by using the keynotes to "get to yes."

Participants use the keynotes to record their ideas and post them on an easel pad. Rules are that they have 10 minutes to generate a minimum of 15 ideas for their group. Nagle's primary rule is : *As soon as you think it, ink it!* No editing or censoring is allowed and quantity is valued over quality. One of his groups came up with 108 ideas in 10 minutes! Once the ideas are generated, the keynotes facilitate the clustering of ideas for organization and adjustments.

Nagle states, "The key is that the group's energy is going toward the problem. They sit around a flip chart or legal pad so they are literally facing the problem rather than confronting each other. The keynotes help make intangible ideas a little more tangible and then they can be prioritized and rearranged . . . they're like chess pieces that can be moved.

"One phenomenon I discovered during a keynoting session recently," states Nagle, "is that the size of the board influences the number of ideas generated. When people use a limited-sized board — like a flip chart pad — they generate fewer ideas than when they use a wide open board with an unlimited field of vision." Most office supply stores now sell eight-foot rolls of white paper which are ideal for hanging on a "thinking wall."

Tom McDaniel with Hughes Technical Management Systems reports that they regularly put proposals through a "wall review." McDaniel states, "We put the proposal on the wall and have people add comments with sticky notes. The comments and comments-on-comments lead to a much better proposal . . . and more wins!"

Think of an instance where brainstorming with sticky notes might be effective for you. Try it!

The Question Is the Key

Patti Konsti, a 3M education specialist who frequently facilitates brainstorming sessions using Post-it™ notes explains the process she uses, "The question is the key. The problem or opportunity needs to be drafted or written and placed in a spot visible to all — on an easel pad, on an overhead projector or handed out to each participant. How it's drafted is important because the doors need to be left open as much as possible and the group needs to thoroughly understand the question or the problem. Enough information must be provided for people to understand what it is that they are being asked to do . . . without leading them into any solution or any area of thinking.

"People love the process of brainstorming with Post-it™ notes because they get results," explains Konsti. "In a one hour meeting, they get the results that might have taken several hours to get with more typical methods. This process reduces the time needed for problem solving by 75-80 percent. We start with silent brainstorming — each person has a pad of Post-it™ notes and writes an idea down on each sheet. This is a critical part of the process especially for the more introverted members of the group because it gives people a chance to reflect. People can see their ideas, in their own handwriting, becoming part of the process. They feel connected to the process."

Konsti generally concludes her sessions by having the group do "flag voting." Another 3M product — Post-it Tape Flags™ — are given to each participant (generally 3-5 flags) and each person uses the flags to vote for the best ideas.

Make It Fun

Probably the number one clue that creativity and transformation thinking are happening is laughter. Laughter and fun free the mind from barriers and restrictions.

Whenever possible do whatever you can to make your thinking sessions fun. Remember what Anarcharsis said in 600 B.C. — *Play so that you may be serious.* Here are just a few ideas:

❐ Have everyone bring water pistols to your meetings — anyone who makes a negative comment gets shot (several organizations actually do this). Or use nerf balls to throw at people who get long-winded or negative.

❐ Have everyone wear silly hats or banana noses.

❐ Do some ridiculous or childish activity as a warm-up.

❐ Tell a joke.

❐ Play a game or solve a puzzle.

❐ Have cookies and milk ... or other more adult snacks if you must.

❐ Do a guided imagery.

❐ Generate Stupid and Ridiculous ideas — When you give people permission to be "stupid and ridiculous," they start to say whatever comes into their minds. They loosen up and look for things that obviously wouldn't work. Or would they?

The University Medical Center in Jacksonville, Florida, was trying to find ways to increase the effectiveness of their quality program. After brainstorming in a normal fashion for awhile, participants decided to try being stupid and ridiculous. Among the ideas they generated were:
- hire the ex-CEO of AT&T Universal Card Service (a 1992 Malcolm Baldrige Quality Award winner)
- give every employee a $1,000 raise
- send 100 employees to a resort for planning
- cross-train 100 employees for every hospital job
- provide 24 hours of Quality training for every employee
- give everyone a promotion
- have management stay home

Most of these ideas brought a lot of laughter but when the group hit the idea of having management stay home, they started to play with it and bounce around on it. They used "what if?" to develop possibilities which included:

❐ What if managers stayed home for one day each month?
Responses: . . . We'd love it!
. . . We could rest!
. . . We could take our computers home and work on a Quality plan for our departments.

❐ What if we let employees "walk in our shoes" while we were out?
Response: . . . They could run the departments for us.

❐ What would happen if we got out of the way and let them do their jobs?

❐ What if each of us used the day to observe another organization known for high quality and service?

❐ What if we used that day as an education day?
Response: . . . We could go to a seminar or workshop.

By lightening up and allowing "stupid and ridiculous" ideas to be voiced, they generated some ideas that were anything but "stupid and ridiculous."

Think of your last planning session, meeting or idea generation event. How much laughter did you hear? Did you have fun? Was it effective? What could you do to reduce tension and make it more fun?

Thinking on Your Feet

❖
Stand up!

Dr. Max Vercruyssen, assistant professor of human factors at the University of Southern California, gave one hundred adults of all ages a set of computer tasks to perform for 15 minutes . . . some while standing . . . some while sitting. "The performance ratings ranged from 5 percent to 30 percent higher for the subjects while they were standing," reported Dr. Vercruyssen.

Although the researchers do not know why we think better on our feet, they theorize that our body and our brain are more poised for action when standing. Based on this study, Dr. Vercruyssen recommends that we occasionally stand up when doing work that requires mental activity.

Groups can take advantage of this physical thinking phenomenon by having people stand while they are brainstorming or working through a thinking process. Having the group stand increases physical energy, prevents doodling or other inattentive activities, stimulates participation and allows people to move around and see the information from different angles.

The Transformation Thinking Basic Four

Thinking together is a natural process but it is not one that happens naturally. To get the most from your group thinking processes, keep these four fundamentals in mind:

❏ **participation** — Make sure everyone participates; do not allow anyone to withdraw from the group.

❏ **visual** — Present information visually. Use color, symbols, graphs, charts and other visual tools to make the information meaningful. If someone goes off on a long-winded tangent, have them summarize their point in a drawing or a short statement that can be posted on the easel pad or whiteboard.

❏ **moveable** — Make the information moveable. Use sticky notes or index cards to capture information or ideas in a way that allows them to be rearranged.

❏ **fun** — Lighten up; laugh, have fun, play with your ideas. You can always seriously evaluate them later.

Which of the four transformation thinking basics do you need most in your organization? How can you get started? What can you do today?

Even once you've learned to think together effectively using the four basic principles of transformation thinking, there are several pitfalls that often sabotage the thinking process. The next chapter will show you how to avoid the most common thinking pitfalls.

Chapter Mindmap

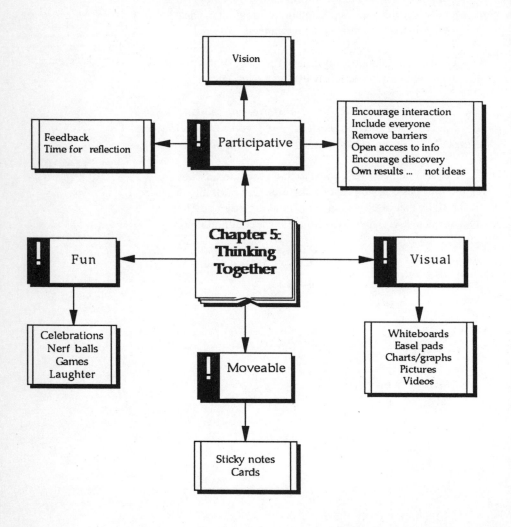

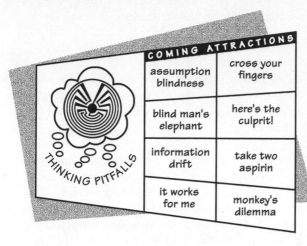

CHAPTER 6

EIGHT THINKING PITFALLS TO AVOID

❖ **Week 1**: Monthly financials have just come out for the Small Software Co. They show an unexpected loss. You're the CEO and as you look at the financials you notice that sales are down sharply. In the financial review meeting, you ask why and here's the responses:

Marketing manager: This is the first month that the company ad didn't show up in the computer buyers' guide due to a cost cutting decision made at budget time.

Sales manager: The recession is making everyone cut back or delay spending.

Customer service manager: Returns are up and there may be a problem with product quality.

After considerable discussion, the executive committee decides to reinstate the advertising budget for the buyers' guide and appoint a task force to investigate software problems.

❖ **Week 2:** The major account salesperson returns from a trip and reports that the company's largest customer had an internal hardware problem which caused them to cancel their previous month's standard order and actually return product. You have the controller analyze the impact of that action on sales and she determines that the cancellation caused the fluctuation in sales and returns. Her study shows that sales to other customers were actually higher for the month.

The executive committee meets and decides to reverse the decision to reinstate the advertising in the buyers' guide and also decides that the software task force can be disbanded.

❖ **Week 3:** The customer service manager completes an analysis of complaints and presents a report showing that although the total level of complaints are about normal, there is a 50% increase in complaints on the company's newest product. About this same time, the marketing manager presents an analysis showing that the buyer's guide has generated over 20% of the sales for the past six months and without it, sales may plummet.

The executive committee forms an emergency task force to look into the problems with the new product and decides to re-reinstate the advertising in the buyers' guide.

❖ **Week 4:** The controller finishes a profitability-by-product-line report that shows the new product line costs far exceeding revenue and that the bad debt costs on the business generated by the buyer's guide are higher than the gross margins on the product.

The executive committee cancels the buyers' guide advertising, disbands the task force, shuts down the new product line and cancels all future meetings!

Sound familiar? . . . frustrating? While this is a fictitious, condensed version of life in the executive lane, it also represents reality that happens all too often.

Universal Fallibility

❖
We can't know everything.

Jim Cathcart, in his book *The Acorn Principle* explains a principle he calls "Universal Fallibility." The principle states: *We can never know all there is to know about anything . . . let alone everything.* Our thinking is guided by the information we receive and the order in which we receive it. If we'd had the benefit of the controller's report in Week 1 instead of Week 4, we wouldn't have made the frustrating series of flip-flops.

In 1980, IBM passed up the opportunity to buy the DOS software from Bill Gates for about $75,000. In 1986, they turned down the opportunity to buy 10% of Microsoft for around $70 million and missed an investment that was worth over $2.5 billion by late 1993. In hindsight we can all recognize the lost opportunities in those decisions. At the time they probably looked extremely reasonable.

Keep in mind there is always the possibility that a new piece of information will show up that will render your most recent decision completely stupid. Regardless of what you do or how you try to protect yourself, that possibility will always be there. The moral is to do as much as possible to prevent that possibility, to keep a large store of humility on file, . . . and to be as kind as possible to others when their moment of fallibility shows up.

What decisions are you facing? Do you recognize the fallibility of your information and assumptions? How can you "hedge your bets?"

Pitfalls to Avoid

With the brilliance of hindsight, let's examine some of the problems the executive committee faced and identify eight pitfalls they might have avoided.

Assumption Blindness: We all know the hazards of making assumptions but the problem is that they're so natural, we often don't even recognize that we're making them. For instance in Week 1 our executive committee made the assumption that the drop in sales was caused by eliminating the advertising in the buyers' guide. They further assumed that the best way to boost sales was to put the ad back.

In the Week 2 meeting, they assumed that since returns were at a constant level, there was nothing to worry about so they could disband the task force. Two hundred pound giant pandas weigh only a few ounces when they're born. Your "constant level" returns could contain the seeds of a huge problem.

111

In the Week 3 meeting, the executive committee assumed that all sales are good sales.

In Week 4, the underlying assumption was that a product whose costs exceed revenue is a bad product and should be terminated. While true in most cases, there are some cases where that is not true; e.g. loss leaders, products that generate enormous follow-on business, new products where the costs will drop drastically, or products where it makes sense to "buy" into the market.

In the mid-80s, Coca-Cola Corporation was crazed by taste tests sponsored by Pepsi that proved that more people preferred the sweeter taste of Pepsi to the zippier taste of Coke. Visions of Pepsi becoming the number one soft drink sent grown men into a tailspin that resulted in a frantic search for a "new and better" Coke. Millions of dollars and thousands of taste tests later, the new Coke was introduced with all the fanfare of a guaranteed cure for cancer. And the rest is history. Irate Coke drinkers reacted with a militant fury that rocked the business world and eventually brought Coca-Cola to its knees . . . and to a red-faced resurrection of "Classic Coke." The assumptions that created this tempest in a Coke bottle? That Coca-Cola had to be the "Number 1" soft drink and that Coke fans would willingly embrace the new "taste tested" cola.

> **Cure for Assumption Blindness:** Questions . . . especially "Why?" Spend some time trying to identify the assumptions being made. Ask why things are the way they are.

The Blind Man's Elephant: An old story tells about three blind men who were "shown" an elephant. The first blind man touched the tip of the elephant's tail and said, "Ah, this is a small, fuzzy animal." The second man touched the broad, rough side of the elephant and said, "No, this is a big, flat animal . . . like a wall." Holding the elephant's trunk, the third man said, "You're both wrong, an elephant is round . . . like a big snake."

We have a tendency to think that what we see (or perceive through our other senses) is all there is. We look at a piece of the puzzle rather than the entire system. As the great psychologist, Abraham Maslow, said: *A man with a hammer sees every problem as a nail.* That's the way we operate: to a training person, every organizational problem relates to a need for training; to a marketing person, every problem revolves around marketing, and so on.

Our software company's executive committee did this from the very beginning. When they noticed that sales were down, they focused on one primary element of sales — the marketing person's comment about the discontinued advertising in the buyers' guide.

Joe McIlvaine, former general manager for the San Diego Padre's ran into the "blind man's elephant" during a game toward the end of the 1992 baseball season. McIlvaine had helped put together a brilliant team, and for the first time in years it looked like they had a shot at the pennant. Fans were going crazy and player morale was higher than it had ever been.

Toward the end of the season, one of the owners was sitting with McIlvaine in his box and commented, "Can you imagine what will happen if we win this thing? Our payroll will go out of sight!"

In the final weeks of a close pennant race, one of the owners saw the possible win only as additional pressure on salary expenses! McIlvaine knew then that trouble was coming. As soon as the season ended, the club began dumping it's top, highly paid talent and refused to talk to anyone with a salary over $400,000! Baseball's minimum major league salary at that time was $109,000; so it was extremely hard to find many people to talk to in the under $400,000 range. By the end of the 1993 season, the club that had been a top contender had traded away so many of its star players that it trailed far behind the Denver Rockies, the league's new expansion team.

The Padre owners looked at a baseball club and saw only soaring salaries. They reacted to that one element and started chopping off million dollar players. Fans became more than angry . . . they began to take action. A class-action suit was filed against the owners and season ticket sales were off 30%. Player morale plummeted as the few remaining veterans wondered who was next and the dismantling of the team became the season's top baseball scandal.

This version of the "blind man's elephant" is also known as "bottom line blindness," the tendency to equate an organization with its bottom line. It happened to GM in the 1970s when it said it wasn't in the business of making cars, it was in the business of making profits. As a result of this thinking pitfall, GM made neither very well.

> **Cure for The Blind Man's Elephant:** Questions such as Are we sure we have all the pieces? Are we looking at the total system? What are all the possible causes of this problem? What other elements might be involved?

Information Drift: Making general conclusions based on incomplete or random information. Roger Dawson, in his audio-tape series, *Confident Decision Making* calls this pitfall "information drift" because, if we don't understand it and correct for it, we can drift completely off course. According to Dawson the eight major causes of information drift are:

❐ Acting on information that's readily available rather than looking at the entire system or determining what information is needed.

❐ Seeing the information in terms of personal interests or experiences.

❐ Rejecting information that conflicts with our beliefs.

❐ Our inability to recall information completely and accurately.

❐ Selectively acquiring information that appeals to our interests.

❐ Locking into the first idea or opinion presented.

❐ Acting on the most recent information.

❐ Emphasizing information that supports our opinions or positions rather than objectively reviewing all information.

Too often we act on a few complaints, comments or suggestions, hearing what we want to hear or what we think is the answer and changing directions or making decisions based on distorted information rather than facts. Charlie Hess, the co-founder and partner of Inferential Focus, a high powered trend spotting futurist consulting firm, says, "One robin does not make a spring." His firm analyzes over 300 magazines and newspapers to spot trends. Their rule is that it takes 3-5 events to create an inference. That inference is then analyzed to determine whether or not it is the harbinger of a trend.

> **Cure for Information Drift:** Try to disconnect personal interests, opinions and experiences from information. Look for holes in the information. Ask what other information you need before taking action.

It Works for Me: Adopting solutions without looking at the impact to others. For instance, assume you manufacture computers and your near year-end numbers are looking pretty peaked. You turn to your vp of marketing and say, "We've got to get the numbers up. Move some product!" She rushes out the door and you lean back in your chair — problem solved. The marketing vp is a human dynamo and by the time the year ends, sales are up 10% over last year and profits look good. The stock price ticks up a few points; the board of directors gives you a fat bonus; all is well.

Well, maybe. There are rumblings in the hinterlands. In an overcrowded warehouse in Paducah, an inexperienced forklift operator moving a pallet of your computers for the third time drops the whole load. Two dealers in Dallas who stocked up on your year-end specials ran out of cash and filed Chapter 11. Customer complaints are up because the operating system shipped with the computer is out-of-date. Returns are up 20% and sales for the new year seem to have mysteriously plummeted.

This particular example of the "It Works for Me" pitfall is so prevalent it has an official name — trade loading. Rather than cut their production, manufacturers offer special incentives to retailers to load up on product. The product winds up sitting in warehouses, gathering dust on shelves and getting shop worn from frequent handling. One rather startling statistic related to this practice in the food industry is that the average grocery product takes 84 days to travel from factory floor to store shelf. Think about that the next time you open a box of crackers! Some estimates say this practice adds up to $400 billion to our grocery bills.

While trade loading fixed the computer manufacturer's immediate problem, it obviously doesn't work for everyone else.

It's a short-term fix that makes the problem worse in the long-run. The manufacturer forgets who his customers are and doesn't keep the entire sales cycle in view. To move product in a way that works for everyone requires looking for a way to pull the product through the entire system rather than push it off to the next level of the sales cycle!

Here's another example of "It works for me.": One recent winter in the Emmental region of Switzerland, consternation swept through the Swiss cheese industry. The winter cheeses were growing bigger and bigger, pushing against their rinds and expanding to an unusual girth. For the Swiss, this was a significant problem — their packing machines wouldn't handle the giant cheeses plus there was a nagging suspicion that the bulging cheeses might be tainted.

When the cheese makers sliced into the cheeses, they found holes that were twice the normal size. Swiss scientists rushed in to study the problem and the trail led to the Milk Research Institute which provided the bacteria cultures that transform milk to cheese. The institute had fiddled with the culture formula. By not thinking about the impact of their fiddling on the manufacturing processes of the cheese makers, the institute set off a wave of hysteria and caused the entire batch of winter cheeses to be turned into cheese spread.

> **Cure for It Works for Me:** Look at who might be impacted by your decisions or actions. Ideally, make all the affected parties part of the decision process.

Cross Your Fingers — Hoping that something works rather than thinking through all the possible ramifications if it doesn't and creating back-up plans.

Contingency planning isn't an idle activity for organizations with time to spare . . . it's a way of thinking. It goes back to the concept of universal fallibility: no matter how certain you think you are, you can never know everything about anything . . . therefore, you could be wrong. If you could be wrong, then making back-up plans is not just a nice idea, it's crazy not to. When Federal Express built their new computer center in Memphis, Tennessee, they put in state-of-the-art (read expensive) earthquake protection. While Memphis isn't exactly earthquake-central, historically a few major quakes have rocked the area and the risk of having their computer center knocked out was greater than the cost of the protection.

> **Cure for Cross Your Fingers:** Ask yourself, "What could go wrong?" Then develop a plan for that. Then ask yourself, "What else could go wrong?" For more important decisions, ask others the same question. For very important decisions, hire experts and ask them that question.

Here's the Culprit! — Looking for one broken part, system, or person in a complex "mess" that has a multitude of separate problems. We love to find the one person or thing to blame because we can "fix" that and move on. The software company's executive committee jumped on the ad in the buyers' guide as the cause of the sales drop. It was a quick fix and they could move on with a sense of satisfaction of having solved the problem. That's what managers get paid for: making quick decisions and solving problems. Or at least that's the way it used to be.

When Mike Walsh, CEO of Union Pacific Railroad, learned that there were errors on 18% of the bills being sent to customers, he set up a special team to investigate the problem. They found 20 different causes spread across every department of the organization. Twenty teams were set up to address each of the identified problems. This is a much longer and messier process than the "quick fix" but most organizational problems don't have a single cause and any "quick fix" will have, at best, a temporary, partial effect.

> **Cure for Here's the Culprit!:** Chapter 9 will introduce you to "mess mapping," a process that will help you avoid the quick-fix mentality or trying to find one person or thing to blame.

Take Two Aspirin — The tendency to solve a symptom rather than the actual cause of the problem. A drop in sales or profit is a symptom; a decrease in quality is a symptom; an increase in customer complaints is a symptom. Trying to fix a symptom is like a doctor prescribing drugs before diagnosing the illness . . . in some quarters that's called malpractice. There's a lot of things you can do that are like taking two aspirins . . . they make the pain go away. And, sometimes the pain stays away if there's no serious underlying problem. There's nothing wrong with aspirin as long as you know that you're just killing the pain and don't begin to think you're curing the disease.

Recently the community of Huntington Beach, California, got tired of complaints by irritable citizens who were being kept awake by noisy, late night parties on the beach. To solve the problem, they banned beach usage after 10:00 p.m. Did this solve the problem? Not likely. Young people with excess energy and no place to go aren't going to just say, "Oh, we can't party at the beach anymore so I guess we'll just go home and go to bed." They'll just get back in their cars and move the problem somewhere else. The problem wasn't the noisy beach . . . but rather the lack of safe, acceptable socialization outlets for young people who need to be with each other but aren't old enough to have their own place.

Not only did Huntington Beach solve a symptom rather than a problem, they also fell into the "It works for me" syndrome. They got rid of citizen complaints about noisy beach parties but how many other beach lovers are now also deprived of their moonlit walks? And, which other community now has the problem?

> **Cure for Take Two Aspirin:** Ask yourself, "What's causing this?" Look for the underlying problem. "Mess mapping" in Chapter 9 will help you look beyond symptoms to the actual problems.

Monkey's Dilemma — The unwillingness to let go of something even when holding on can only spell failure. When a monkey reaches into a jar and grabs a fistful of nuts, he's delighted because he's got what he wants in his hand. When he can't get his enlarged fist out of the jar, he winds up not getting the nuts in the jar or the ones that he could get by going outside and climbing the nut tree. If he would just let go of the nuts in the jar, he also might stumble onto the idea of turning the jar upside down and pouring the nuts out! The "fistful of nuts" syndrome is one of the main reasons that breakthroughs seldom come from the most logical place. Microcomputers weren't invented by a major computer manufacturer; cellular phones didn't come from AT&T; railroads, the major transportation system of yesterday, didn't invent airplanes, the major transportation system of today. It's very difficult to let go of something tangible to look for new possibilities.

This pitfall is strongly related to the idea that "It worked yesterday!" In our rapidly changing world, what worked yesterday may be exactly the wrong thing for today. We can't turn back the clock and it doesn't do much good to pine for the "good old days." We have to be willing to look objectively at what we're doing and if something isn't working, let it go and look for a better way.

> **Cure for A Fistful of Nuts** — Regularly review all actions, even the ones that seem to be successful, to see if they're still working or if there might be a better response to today's problems.

Which of these pitfalls is most prevalent in your organization? Are there any that you do a great job of avoiding? How can you begin to get people more aware of these pitfalls?

There is nothing complicated about Transformation Thinking . . . it doesn't take fancy equipment or advanced degrees. It does require an understanding of how our mind works and a good grasp of group dynamics. It also requires a willingness to do things differently than they were done yesterday and a respect for the potential and capabilities that each individual person brings to an organization.

The next section will show you how to apply Transformation Thinking to specific organizational tasks by using powerful thinking tools.

Chapter Mindmap

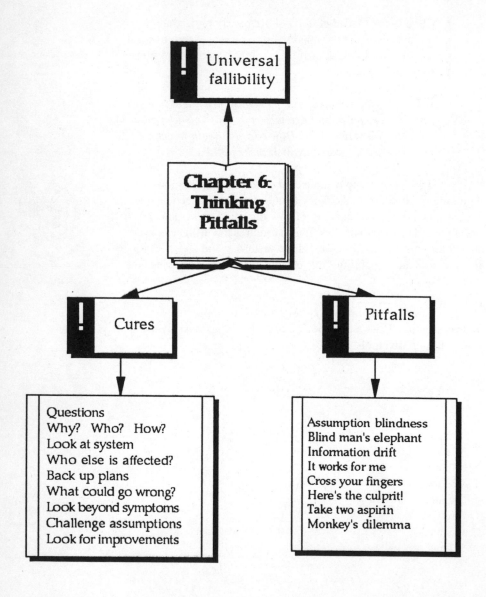

POWER THINKING TOOLS

Everything humankind has invented —
from the wheel to New Age philosophies —
began with our collective creative abilities.
And, barring a messiah or a visit from an ET,
all of the advances created in the future —
whether for good or for bad —
will begin with this same creative process.

Understanding and nurturing creative thinking
is one of the most important steps we can take
to improve ourselves and our world.
— Marsh Fisher, CEO, FisherIdea Systems

A New Look for an Old Church

On the edge of The Loop in Chicago, Old St. Patrick's Church had been left behind by suburban flight. By 1983 when Rev. Jack Wall took over, it was down to four registered members. With no residential neighborhood to draw from, Rev.Wall was forced to look for other possibilities. He decided to focus on spirituality in work life and began scheduling weekday masses before work and during lunchtimes. Rev. Wall asked people what they wanted and then found ways to let them get involved in providing it.

In order to introduce people to the new programs, the church threw a block party and sent flyers to the businesses in the neighborhood. Uncertain as to how many people might show up, they planned for a thousand and were overwhelmed when more than five thousand people arrived! Today the registered membership at the church is more than 1,500 but that statistic tells only part of the story. Because the church is located in a predominantly commercial district, most of the people involved with it live some distance away. For most, it makes sense for them to maintain their church membership in their home parish. An associate member program was initiated as a way to allow these people to be a part of St. Patrick's without switching their membership. There are now over 11,500 associate members. However, the figure Rev. Wall is most proud of is the 2,500 volunteers who work with the multitude of programs offered by the church! St. Patrick's found a way to let people give themselves what they want and what they need. Using what most organizations call empowerment, St. Patrick's transformed itself.

Transformation Tasks

III

Transformation of an organization is never a one-shot, quick-fix, over-and-done-with type of process. It's a never-ending, all-encompassing, everyone's involved, everything's important, it-can-always-be-better attitude. It's not enough to teach people how to solve problems or even how to have a quality process that focuses on continuous improvement. The organization that wants to encourage and stimulate transformation must provide its associates with powerful thinking tools, teach them how to use those tools in a wide variety of tasks, and create an environment of vision and empowerment that encourages action.

Here are the most common thinking tasks performed in a transformation environment:

❐ **Making things better:** A transformation environment is always looking for ways to make things better. There is an attitude of curiosity and an acceptance of ideas regardless of their source. People are willing to learn from customers, competitors, other industries, and each other regardless of rank, longevity, educational achievements or level of expertise. Making things better includes process improvement and problem solving.

❏ **Making leaps:** Sometimes making things better isn't enough . . . we need to "boldly go where no man has gone before." We need to recognize shifts in technology, consumer needs, expectations and directions. We need to let go of the past and step into the future . . . a step that is often hazardous or uncertain at best. Making leaps through innovation and creativity requires outstanding idea generation skills.

❏ **Consensus decision making:** Transformation environments acknowledge the contribution of every member of the organization and recognize the importance of "buy-in." They develop decision making processes that promote acceptance and agreement, facilitate communication and stimulate action.

❏ **Project management:** In a transformation environment the people who will manage and implement the project are involved from the inception. Therefore, management of the project is more about communication, tracking results and providing feedback than about motivating or directing.

❏ **Training:** A transformation environment is a learning and thinking environment. Training is a continuing activity, whether it's through formal training programs or individual-to-individual sharing of information, skills and techniques.

❏ **Communication:** Communication is the bloodstream of an organization. It carries the nutrients needed for life in every cell and fiber of the operation. If communication is blocked even temporarily, the organization will begin to die. Transformation requires a high level of co-active (open, inclusive, multi-sensory) communication.

Transformation thinking tasks are cross-functional. They are just as important to accounting as they are to sales and marketing, just as critical to the data entry crew as to the design engineers. Unfortunately, these thinking tasks are seldom taught in our schools and colleges. Fortunately, they are becoming an increasingly important part of training programs in corporate America.

Pizza Boxes and Pitfalls

Domino's Pizza cut the corners off their pizza boxes to save money and wound up delivering a hotter pizza and saving 470,000 trees in four years!

Domino's definitely made things better but it isn't always easy. Ken Zion was in package design with Stone Container when he discovered a way to make a less expensive pizza box for Domino's. The octagonal shape eliminated 10 percent of the material used simply by cutting off the corners. This new shape held round pizzas in place better and helped retain heat by eliminating the corner dead spaces. But Domino's is a time-sensitive operation, committed to delivering all pizzas within 30 minutes. To save time, the pizza was cut in the box and the new box shape required a change in operations. Jim Caldwell, purchasing director for Domino's states, "For the first six months after we introduced the box, our phone rang off the hook with complaints from operations."

Domino's pizza box illustrates a typical change situation that backfires at implementation:

Good Idea: Domino's was open to an idea that came from a supplier.

Not-so-good Implementation: All the "players" weren't involved. The people out in the field who have to work with an eye on the clock weren't delighted by the change in their operations. Therefore, the change took a lot more salesmanship and "management."

Domino's management showed a trace of the thinking pitfall "It Works for Me" as they adopted a change which saved them money but adversely impacted (at least in the short-run) another segment of the operation. The reality is that we will seldom do everything right but the more we can be aware of the thinking pitfalls and the dynamics of change, the closer we will come to creating a transformation environment.

Transformation Tasks and Tools

Just as a carpenter wouldn't use a sledgehammer on a delicate piece of furniture, some thinking tools are more appropriate for some tasks than others. It's important to understand your mission so that you can choose the tasks that will accomplish the goal and select the thinking tool which best fits those tasks.

Transformation Tasks & Tools

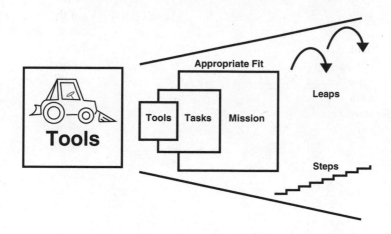

III

The following chapters give you several power thinking tools which can be used to create transformation in any organization. Some tools are better for specific tasks and some can be combined when performing certain tasks. Each chapter will identify the tasks most appropriate for the specific tool.

COMING ATTRACTIONS

commitment	future wheels
group make-up	guidelines
energy management	killer phrases
clustering	
conformity pressures	idea words

TOOL:
BETTER
BRAINSTORMING

Tasks: Making things better
Making leaps
Training
Communication

Ordinary people are an extraordinary source
of information about the real world.
— David Angus, Gary Frank, Bob Rehm
from **Discovering Common Ground** *by Marvin R. Weisbord*

It's a typical situation — a company needs a new idea for a product or service. Or they need a way to boost sales, improve customer relations or increase employee morale. Several people go into a conference room and "brainstorm" for an hour and then leave, often feeling frustrated and disappointed.

Doug Hall, president of Richard Saunders, Inc. (Richard Saunders is the pen name used by Benjamin Franklin for *Poor Richard's Almanac*), believes there is a better way and recent university studies have validated his ideas. Instead of just having people sit in a windowless conference room and "brain-drain" (Hall's term), he takes them to the Eureka!® Mansion where they participate in the Eureka! Stimulus Process™. Eureka! Mansion is an adult-child's fantasy world. Located on 6 1/2 acres near

Cincinnati, the 150-year-old Greek Revival home is designed for fun. Among the adult toys available to relax and stimulate corporate brains are a half mile off-road go-cart track, an imported white sand volleyball court, an adult size "monster" playground, three "wicked-cool" pinball machines and an arsenal of foam bows and arrows, balls, frisbees, Play-doh, and other assorted toys. Corporate clients are greeted with a genuine red carpet, a Dixie-land jazz band and the insistence that they must have fun.

Hall, the stimulus behind Eureka! Mansion, is a modern-day, Ben Franklin–type inventor with an enviable track record of helping his clients develop products. He helped launch Crystal Pepsi, Eveready Battery Co.'s Green Powerbattery and dozens of other products. A *Wall Street Journal* article about Hall's approach to creativity states, "Mr. Hall's clients appear willing to take that risk (the short life-span of most new products). PepsiCo Inc., Nike, Walt Disney, and Southwestern Bell Corp are among the major companies paying between $20,000 and $120,000 per project for his new product assistance. Satisfied clients say that he often beats their product-development teams because he can generate scores of ideas in a month or less."

Van Melle Candy Company of Holland wanted to find a new candy so Hall took the Eureka! Stimulus process to a posh hotel at the northern end of the Netherlands. The idea generation team gathered together but they needed a stimulus according to Hall's creativity formula — $E = (S + B.O.S.)^f$. (Translation: Idea Generation = Stimulus plus Brain Operating System all raised to the fun power.) To find their stimulus, someone reached into a bag full of toys and pulled out a toy gun. That stimulus set them off on thoughts that included: candy that could be shot into mouths, silver bullets ala the Lone Ranger, candy capsules that break and look like blood, making a candy that tastes ugly, a fire ball candy, a Russian roulette candy with surprises inside. And so it went.

Arthur VanGundy, Ph.D., communication professor at the University of Oklahoma, recently completed a study to document the effectiveness of variations in the brainstorming process. Thirty groups worked on a real business project for Frito-Lay, using brainstorming variations ranging from a group receiving no instruction other than to generate ideas about the project, to a group that used the Eureka! Stimulus Response™ method. The study showed that the Eureka! Stimulus Response method generated 10 times as many ideas as brain-draining and five times as many ideas with strong market potential (as judged by Frito-Lay). The study verifies Hall's position that adding stimulus techniques to a collection of different personal styles (brain operating systems) creates greater mental activity with new connections and more ideas.

Another result of the study was a verification of the importance of the standard brainstorming "rules" (no judgment, quantity wanted, wild ideas accepted, and "bouncing" off other ideas). The group that was presented with these rules generated twice as many ideas as the group that did not have the rules emphasized.

And what was the outcome of the candy invention process? . . . A candy called G.U.T.S., short for Great Unbelievable Tasting Sweets. Some of the candies in each box are red hots, the rest are fruity sweet.

When people get together to think, whether it's a problem solving session or to generate ideas for a new product or service, they generally call what they're doing brainstorming. Often what they're doing is actually brain-draining and they wind up disappointed in the results.

Brainstorming isn't difficult or complicated but it does require an understanding of the qualities of the "two thinkers" (see Chapter 4), a knowledge of how to stimulate divergent thinking (see Chapter 5), and a good grasp of group dynamics.

We've already discussed divergent thinking and provided several "stimulators" so this chapter will focus on the group processes that are critical to brainstorming and all group thinking sessions. In the past few years many studies have been done on brainstorming. These studies found three conditions that affect the quality of the brainstorming sessions:

Group commitment — Groups that are committed and interested in the outcome of the brainstorming session are more productive than groups that have little investment in the results.

Group makeup — Diverse groups representing different backgrounds, skills, organizational levels, and points of view are more productive than homogeneous groups.

Uniformity Pressures — All groups exert a pressure toward uniformity on its members. For a brainstorming session to be effective, these pressures must be minimized. Techniques for reducing uniformity pressures include:

❏ **Allowing time for individual idea generation.** Before beginning the brainstorming session, allow 3-5 minutes for individual brainstorming. Mindmapping (Chapter 12) is an excellent technique to help people start to form their own thoughts. This individual thinking time helps prevent a follow-the-leader type of thought process.

❏ **Breaking the group into small groups of 3-4.** People who are shy or at lower levels in the organization will feel much more comfortable expressing their opinions in a small group. Additionally, if someone is not participating, it becomes very evident in a small group and the group can encourage the non-participator.

❏ **Realigning groups frequently.** Realigning groups gives people more exposure to new ideas and prevents the build-up of group hierarchies. Even in a short workshop, stable groups will develop "roles" . . . this person is the recorder, that person is the presenter, another is the idea generator. Breaking up these role developments, helps keep everyone in the group on the same level of participation and prevents the "familiarity breeds similarity" syndrome where people who spend a lot of time together begin to think alike.

❏ **Asking for "minority" reports.** People often "go along" with a group decision or direction of thinking simply to avoid making waves. Asking for "minority" reports allows people who have second thoughts, reservations or hesitations to make them known. It helps stimulate more divergent thinking.

❏ **Using activities and humor.** Activities that require movement, participation and humor can help break down communication and organizational barriers. When people laugh together or share an activity, they begin to see each other as individuals rather than titles or positions.

Energy Management

Effective brainstorming sessions depend upon the facilitator's ability to manage the group's energy. Group energy acts like adrenalin stimulating ideas and connections that would not be made without it. Here are some effective energy stimulators:

❑ **Use divergence stimulators** — When the flow of ideas begins to lag, use a divergence stimulator to get the group energy moving. Remember that creativity lurks on the bottom so the first time the group "runs out" of ideas probably just means that they have run out of cliche-thinking. Pushing them into a new vein of thought usually results in new ideas and sometimes a golden nugget. Requiring an additional quota of ideas or getting them to think of five "stupid and ridiculous" ideas can start the flow again. (See Chapter 4 for more idea stimulators.)

❑ **Take an in-room break** — Take five minutes and have everyone throw nerf balls around the room, play loud music with a strong beat, have people stretch or do some physical activity, ask for jokes (make restrictions about content if you don't want to listen to off-color or ethnic jokes), bring in children's toys and have people play with them, have a five-minute art contest and post the results, or do anything else you can think of that gets people moving or doing something totally different from what they were doing in the brainstorming session. Then, immediately go back to the brainstorming.

❑ **Alternate small group/large group** — moving back and forth between individuals, small groups and the large group generates energy. The small group provides more safety and freedom and the large group provides diversity with new inputs, ideas and directions.

❑ **Do a sidestep** — Explore a related aspect of the situation. If you were trying to brainstorm ways to improve communication, you might do a sidestep and brainstorm all the possible ways of communicating . . . from smoke signals to e-mail. Or, you might explore ways to communicate without words. What the sidestep is isn't as important as the process of opening up the thinking. Any sidestep that brings more information to the brainstorming process will start the mental processes churning again. If valuable information is generated, post it on the wall and then return to the brainstorming session.

❐ **Use "killer" balls** — Soft, nerf balls can be used in a light-hearted way to help keep people focused, prevent long-winded discussions or digressions, stop judgmental comments or prevent "expert-itis."

Enhanced Brainstorming

Here is an overview of the process you can use to enhance your brainstorming sessions and make them more successful and more productive:

❐ **Set the Stage** — An atmosphere of accepting, freewheeling thinking is the goal. Reassure everyone that this is just the idea generation stage and that ideas will be reviewed later and assessed for reasonableness. Be a little offbeat and humorous.

❐ **Define the objective** — Make sure everyone understands the objective of the session and enough of the background to make a contribution.

❐ **Warm up the group by mindmapping** (Chapter 12) all the desirable outcomes that could happen if the brainstorming session is successful. Have them brainstorm a "perfect world" outcome. This starts to loosen up the thinking process and builds interest in the outcome as people start to see possibilities . . . and see that the door is open to new ideas and directions.

❐ **Start with individuals** — Have each person mindmap ideas on paper. This gets individual thinking started and helps develop a broader base of ideas.

❐ **Move to the small groups** — Have each small group combine ideas and generate as many more ideas as possible. This step may not be necessary if you have six people or less in the brainstorming session.

❐ **Combine ideas** — Combine ideas at the whole group session and use divergent thinking stimulators such as opposites and bouncing to encourage the group to build on the ideas listed.

❐ **Record all ideas** — It's extremely important to record all ideas as they are called out with as little alteration as possible. Ideas are fragile and it's the recorder's job to record them, not change them. Recording the ideas in a mindmapping format helps prevent linear thinking and any semblance of "ranking."

Brainstorm Cards

Another way to generate more ideas is with brainstorm cards. Instead of having people mindmap their ideas initially, give each person a stack of index cards and have them write one idea on each card. Allow about five minutes for this process and then collect the cards and mix them up. Give several cards to each small group and have them use the cards as idea stimulators.

Clustering

Enhanced brainstorming uses three of the four transformation thinking fundamentals: it's visual, participatory and uses humor. However, the information generated in standard brainstorming processes is not moveable. Enter Post-it™ notes. Using these sticky notes as part of the brainstorming process makes the ideas moveable and facilitates the "clustering" of ideas. When ideas are grouped based on common characteristics or themes, an organization and structure begins to arise from the information. More ideas are generated as people begin to see the structure and fill in gaps. A sense of priority or dominance is often revealed as one or more of the clusters claim the energy and interest of the group.

Future Wheels

3M offers a collection of 84 ideas "for teachers by teachers" that show creative uses of Post-it™ notes and other 3M products. The booklet is filled with ideas that could also be used by businesses and other organizations. One idea is "FutureWheels," a method of brainstorming "what if." The "what if" question is written on a Post-it™ and placed in the center of a large piece of paper. Brainstormers write their ideas on smaller notes and put them around the center idea. Again, participants are encouraged to bounce off the ideas of others.

> **Process:** Group develops a "what-if" question, which is written on a Post-it™ note and placed in the center of a large sheet of paper.
>
> Participants spend several minutes writing their ideas on Post-it™ notes, one idea per note.
>
> Ideas are placed around the central question.
>
> Related ideas are clustered together and new ideas are recorded as they occur.
>
> Secondary rounds can use some of the ideas as further "what ifs."

Linda O'Neal, Ph.D., is one of the teachers who suggested ideas for the 3M booklet. She is quoted as saying: *It's vital for effective teachers to find ways to actively involve learners, so they truly make the content their own.* Is it any less vital for members of an organization to "own" the content of decisions and changes in their own organization?

Brainstorming Guidelines:

- ❐ Be light-hearted and humorous whenever possible.
- ❐ Make sure all participants fully understand the objective.
- ❐ Encourage active participation of all members.
- ❐ Develop a high energy, enthusiastic environment.
- ❐ Avoid discussing ideas ... criticizing or complimenting.
- ❐ Encourage wild ideas.
- ❐ Build and expand on the ideas of others.
- ❐ Record all ideas as presented.
- ❐ When ideas slow down, use a stimulator to generate more.
- ❐ Use "killer" balls to stop non-productive activities.
- ❐ Limit comments to 15 seconds.

Killer Phrases

Thanks to Ed Preston (you'll meet him again in Chapter 13) for this list of "killer" phrases. Anyone who hears one of these phrases in a brainstorming session should let loose with a "killer" ball.

It's not in the budget.
We're not ready for that.
Everybody does it this way.
Too hard to administer.
Too theoretical.
Production won't accept it.
Personnel isn't ready for this.
Not timely.
The old people won't use it.
The new people won't understand it.
Takes too much time (work).
Don't move too fast.
Has anyone else ever tried it?
Let's make a market test first.
Let's form a committee.
Won't work in our territory.
Too big (or too small) for us.
We don't have the personnel.
We tried that before.
Too academic.
It's a gimmick.
You'll never sell that to management.
Stretches the imagination too much.
Let's wait and see.
Too much trouble to get started.
It's never been done before.
The union will scream.
Let's put it in writing.

Great Idea Words

Ideas love action and action produces energy. These words are great brainstorming tools to open up thinking to new possibilities. Try putting a *What could we . . . ?* or *How could we . . . ?* in front of each word. *What could we* develop? *How could we* develop . . . ?

Develop	Build	Advance	Broadcast
Form	Transmit	Formulate	Acquire
Devise	Increase	Invent	Intensify
Originate	Magnify	Construct	Constitute
Arrange	Establish	Guide	Manufacture
Activate	Produce	Instruct	Install
Teach	Open	Invest	Set up
Spread	Target	Enlighten	Allocate
Tutor	Focus	Inform	Examine
Construct	Highlight	Appoint	Spotlight
Assign	Aim	Implement	Inspire
Create	Instill	Minimize	Diversify

Brainstorming is the most fundamental group thinking tool. It is the basic process used to stimulate idea generation in any group. Every member of the group brings a unique set of traits, skills and experiences to the session and will, therefore, have a slightly different perception of the subject being brainstormed. These different perspectives bring a richness to the session that could never happen with only one person thinking alone in a room.

The effectiveness of your brainstorming sessions depends on how well you use the fundamentals shown in this chapter. For even more information about Doug Hall's Eureka! Stimulus method and other ideas about creativity see his book *Jump Start Your Brain* (Warner Books, 1995). The next chapter shows you how to use "Brainwriting" to increase the effectiveness of your brainstorming sessions.

Chapter Mindmap

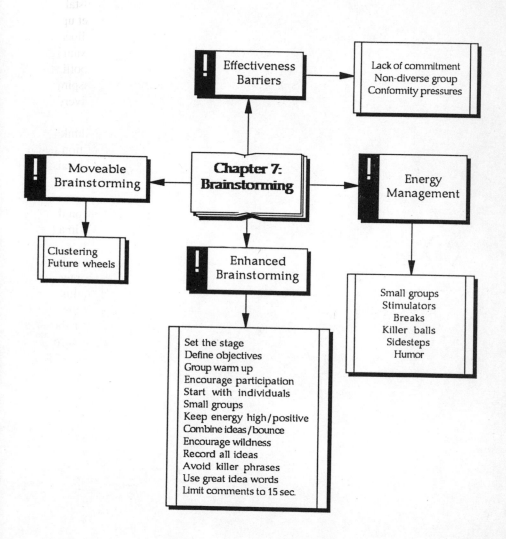

Effectiveness Barriers
Lack of commitment
Non-diverse group
Conformity pressures

Moveable Brainstorming
Clustering
Future wheels

Chapter 7: Brainstorming

Energy Management
Small groups
Stimulators
Breaks
Killer balls
Sidesteps
Humor

Enhanced Brainstorming
Set the stage
Define objectives
Group warm up
Encourage participation
Start with individuals
Small groups
Keep energy high/positive
Combine ideas/bounce
Encourage wildness
Record all ideas
Avoid killer phrases
Use great idea words
Limit comments to 15 sec.

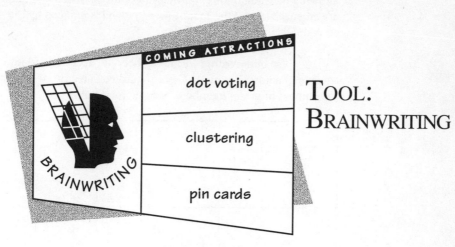

CHAPTER 8

Tasks: Making things better
Making leaps

Perplexity is the beginning of knowledge.
— Kahlil Gibran

One of the most common problems in idea generation sessions is the barrier created by the group hierarchy. The best brainstorming groups are widely diverse, pulling people from different functional areas with different levels of expertise and background. However, these variances can create a barrier as people at the lower levels of the organization are reluctant to speak out for fear of being perceived incompetent or saying something stupid. On the other hand, the people at the higher levels may perceive themselves as "experts" and feel that they need to "lead" the session since they have the most knowledge.

Both responses are counterproductive to a free-wheeling idea generation session. Through the years, some studies have shown that people sitting alone in a room can generate, up to four times more ideas than a group in a brainstorming session. The primary reason for this significant difference is the pressure for conformity that exists in all groups.

Brainwriting is a simple technique that can be used to break through this barrier and stimulate the power of divergent thinking. It is basically a way to brainstorm on paper while allowing the anonymous contribution of ideas. Speed and quantity are emphasized and the fear of being judged is reduced by the anonymous input.

The brainwriting form is a sheet of paper divided into 21 squares (3 across, 7 down). There should be one more sheet than the number of group members. Sample form below:

BRAINWRITING

Process:

❏ **One sheet per person plus one.** Each person receives a brainwriting sheet and one additional sheet is placed in the center of the table where everyone can reach it.

❏ **Three ideas then switch.** Each person writes an idea in the three top-most empty boxes and then places the sheet in the center and takes an available sheet and writes three more ideas on that sheet . . . again in the three top empty boxes.

❏ **List ideas once.** Ideas should only be written down once — they do not have to be written on each sheet.

❏ **Fill all boxes.** The process is continued until all the sheets are filled or until everyone is out of ideas. Have enough blank sheets on hand to keep the process going if there are lots of ideas being generated.

❏ **Bounce.** When ideas begin to slow down, people should scan the previous ideas and try to bounce off of them to create variations and new directions.

❏ **Stimulate when needed.** The brainwriting sheets operate as a thought stimulator by establishing a "quota" of ideas (21 per sheet and a specific number of sheets). If ideas begin to slow down, it may be necessary to use additional stimulators from Chapter 4 such as "Stupid and Ridiculous."

In a few minutes of brainwriting, a group of six people can easily generate 147 ideas (21 ideas per sheet, 7 sheets) . . . then you have to be able to do something with those ideas. There are several ways to "process" the ideas for further development. Here are two that generally lead to additional ideas, maintain the participatory nature of the thinking process and allow a structure to emerge from the ideas:

❏ **Dot Voting** — Each person can vote five (or three) dots per sheet — one dot for the five best ideas or all on one if there is only one idea on the sheet that seems like a potential winner. After voting, the person initials the sheet and passes it on until each person has had a chance to vote on each sheet. The sheets are reviewed and the top vote-getters are culled for further discussion and development.

☐ **Clustering** — The sheets can be cut into the idea squares for clustering. The individual ideas are laid out on a table and people can walk around the table looking at the ideas, moving them into categories and removing redundancies. This process generally generates new ideas or variations so someone should be prepared to capture the new ideas.

Once a structure begins to emerge from the ideas, the idea squares could be taped to Post-it™ notes and placed on a large piece of paper as the beginning of a storyboard or sticky chart.

Pin Cards

Arthur VanGundy, Ph.D., communication professor at the University of Oklahoma, suggests another form of brainwriting that is even simpler than using the brainwriting forms. Everyone in a group is given a supply of index cards. Each person writes an idea on a card and passes it to the right. The cards continue to circulate with people adding ideas to the cards until the group has run out of ideas . . . or the time for the session has expired. The cards create a constant, changing flow of ideas to stimulate new ideas and variations in the next person who receives them. For several other variations of brainwriting, see VanGundy's book *Idea Power.*

Brainwriting is an extremely useful technique for breaking the ice with a group of people who may not be familiar or comfortable with each other. After a few minutes of intense involvement and seeing the ideas generated by others, the process begins to take over and people get caught up in the flurry of idea generation. Barriers are broken down more quickly in a few minutes of brainwriting than often happens in hours of meetings or formalized problem solving sessions.

Chapter Mindmap

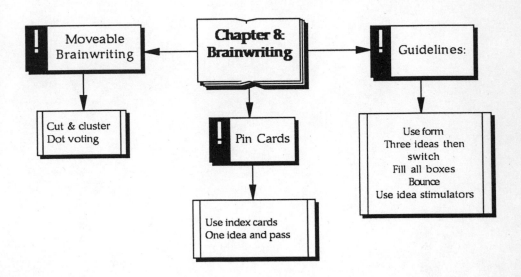

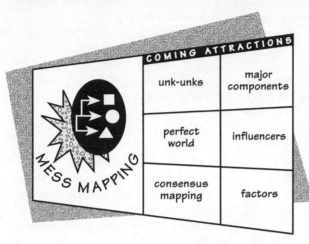

CHAPTER 9

TOOL:
MESS
MAPPING

Tasks: Making things better
Making leaps

Very few management practices I used as an executive in the
1960s or as a consultant in the 1970s work anymore.
— *Marvin R. Weisbord,* Discovering Common Ground

One of the few thinking skills that has been taught fairly
extensively in corporate America is problem solving and there are
many "creative" problem solving models. However, most of these
models tend to depend on linear thinking and while there's nothing
wrong with linear thinking, it provides little opportunity for
transformation. Linear thinking would have us pull the caterpillar
out of its cocoon and get it back on its proper "caterpillar track."
Most of the creative problem solving models are variations on the
following:

- ❏ Define the problem
- ❏ Analyze the problem
- ❏ Generate possible solutions
- ❏ Select the best solution
- ❏ Implement the solution
- ❏ Evaluate success.

Russell Ackoff, professor at the University of
Pennsylvania's Wharton School, says that we don't experience
problems individually but rather as complex systems of interacting
problems . . . what he calls "messes." Systems cannot be taken

145

apart without losing their essential properties so the standard problem solving models have an inherent flaw. As they try to "define the problem" and "analyze the problem," they lose sight of the system.

There is something very one-shot about "problem solving." A "let's fix this problem and get it behind us" approach. Somehow it never seems to work that way. We fix this problem and another one pops up. We solve that problem and get blind-sided by something totally unexpected. We need to stop thinking in terms of one-time activities or solutions and begin to operate more in terms of on-going processes. But, even that is not enough . . . if it were, all we would need to be successful is continuous improvement. But 8-track cartridges got better and CP/M computers (remember them?) got bigger and more powerful. Obviously, it takes something more than problem solving and continuous improvement.

Think back to the early 1900s and imagine Joe Obsolete, CEO of Ajax Buggyworks, confronting the problem of a drop in buggy whip sales. A common customer complaint was that the whips broke in cold weather. Joe calls together his continuous improvement team and they analyze all the possible causes of buggy whip breakage — materials, workmanship, design, etc. It's a good team and soon they have solved the problem and the "new and improved" Ajax buggy whip is ready for the market. Unfortunately the market is gone and all the product improvement in the world will not bring it back.

Beware the Unk-Unks

Thinking about buggy whips, CP/M computers and other obsolete products reminded us of a recent conversation with Dar Richardson, materials manager with EnviroTech in Sacramento. Richardson talks about the "unk-unks" that were discovered during the early days of the space program. In any situation there are things we know and things we don't know. To be more precise, our knowledge (and ignorance) falls into four categories:

- ❐ **Known-knowns** — what we know . . . and know we know
- ❐ **Unknown-knowns** — what we know . . . but aren't aware we know

❑ **Known-unknowns** — what we don't know . . . and know we don't know

❑ **Unknown-unknowns** — what we don't know . . . but aren't aware that we don't know

The last category is the dreaded "unk-unks" — the things we don't know but don't even know we don't know them. They're the things that sneak up on us, the surprises that wreak havoc with our best laid plans. Ajax Buggyworks didn't know that automobiles would replace horses and buggies . . . what's even worse, they didn't know they didn't know, so they weren't planning for possible contingencies.

Any planning or thinking process should keep a visual monument to the "unk-unk" where everyone can see it as a permanent reminder of our universal fallibility. We will never know everything about anything and what's worse, we probably won't even know that we don't know it. As much as possible, we need to probe the unknown-unknowns, but our best bet is to rethink our situation frequently, get input from as many different sources as possible, and be flexible enough to turn on a dime when the inevitable "unk-unk" shows up.

Mess Mapping

Creative problem solving models work — sometimes brilliantly. But we have the same tendency in problem solving that we do in all of our other thinking processes . . . we converge too soon. We are under pressure to define the problem, narrow the focus, make it more specific . . . and do it all right now! Sometimes we have to slow down, stand back and look at the whole mess and say, "What's happening here?"

Borrowing from Ackoff, here is a different approach to problem solving . . . a way to look at a mess divergently.

1. **Identify the mess generally** — e.g. sales are down, the product isn't working, people aren't happy, information isn't flowing. Place a description of the mess in the center of the page page. We'll use the buggy whip example of sales being down for the rest of the process.

2. Perfect World — Look beyond the mess — what would the perfect world without the mess look like? Draw a larger circle around the mess circle and enter the attributes of the perfect world.

> **Examples:** There would be more buggies so people would need more buggy whips. People would only want Ajax whips. The whips would never break so people would pay more for them. The whips would be so good, people would start to use them for other things, so sales would go up again. Costs of materials would drop.

3. Identify major mess components — These are the major elements of the mess. There are usually three to five major areas that need to be considered. Draw these as outlying circles and link back to the central mess.

> **Example components:** the company, the customer, the environment

4. Identify the influencers of each component — this is not cause identification, this is identifying the influencers, whether positive or negative. It's important to keep in mind the point Peter Senge makes in his book, *The Fifth Discipline*: *In systems thinking it is an axiom that every influence is both **cause and effect**. Nothing is ever influenced in just one direction.* List as many as possible and link to component.

Example influencers:

❑ **The company:** product design, suppliers, workforce, management, materials, methods, machinery, financial performance, distribution channels, marketing, sales personnel

❑ **The customer:** the economy, needs, goals, other competitors

❑ **The environment:** economy, technology, demographics

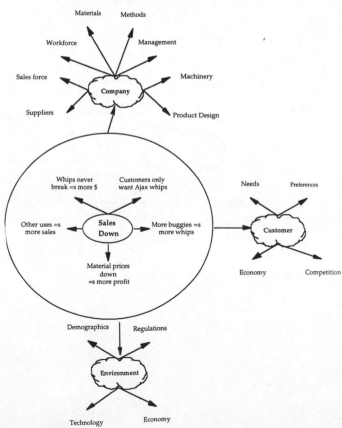

5. Identify important factors or recent changes for each influencer — What factors or recent changes are affecting each influencer. List as many as possible and link to each influencer. This step prompts a questioning process that often reveals trends and new developments.

Example: Ajax Buggyworks could look at itself in-depth and might come up with dozens of problems that could be fixed without ever connecting the drop in sales with a change in customer needs and the environment. However, when it begins to explore influences on the customer and the environment, the chances are very good that it will identify the major challenge presented by the new automobile industry.

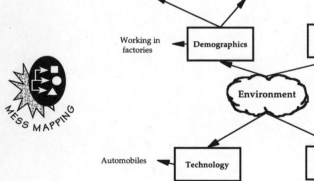

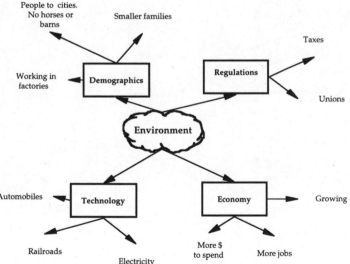

6. Prioritize influencers and changes — Decide which influencers and which factors or changes are having the biggest impact on the mess . . . or which influencers are capable of having the biggest influence. Color code the influencers: Yellow — major impact; Green — moderate impact; Blue — little impact. Then use the same color code to indicate the impact of the changes on the influencer: (If this process is being done on a white board, you will need to change the color codes since yellow has little visual impact on a white board.)

Example of major influencers: People moving to the city and buying automobiles instead of horses.

7. Analyze the major impact items — Are the factors positive or negative? Why did the changes happen? Do they reflect a trend or a short-term event? What are all the possible causes of the change? Color code each item as to its impact.

8. Brainstorm possibilities — Select a primary factor and generate as many ideas, possibilities or solutions as possible.

> **Example:** Ajax Buggyworks realizes that the change in technology and demographics is a long-term trend that will not be influenced by any changes in their present products. They decide to brainstorm ways to transition to a different industry. They might also choose to brainstorm how to maximize profits in a rapidly declining market.

At this point, it may be possible to define a problem that can be addressed with one of the creative problem solving models. Perhaps Ajax has decided that its core competencies revolve around the creation of high-quality leather products. They brainstorm possible leather products and decide to focus on creating leather steering wheel covers. At that point they can define a specific problem and utilize a problem solving model effectively.

Perfect World Expanded

In *Productive Workplaces*, Marvin Weisbord describes a process he calls the Future Search Conference. At a future search conference, people begin by creating an image of the potential, "envisioning what could be instead of lamenting what was." Weisbord states, "When people plan present actions by working backward from what is really desired, they develop energy, enthusiasm, optimism, and high commitment." According to Weisbord, "futuring" focuses attention away from interpersonal relationships and towards the values and dreams held by each person.

George Land, founding partner of the Phoenix-based consulting firm Leadership 2000, calls this process of thinking backwards from a desired ideal, "Working Backward from Perfect" and applies a technology called CoNexus to help facilitate the process. One organization that recently used the technology to achieve dramatic results is Intermedics Orthopedics®, Inc., (IOI) a company of Sulzermedica. IOI is a leading designer, manufacturer and distributor of orthopedic implants for hips, knees and shoulders, located in Austin, Texas, employing approximately 600 people. For the first seven years of IOI's existence, it's primary goal was reaching $100 million in sales.

About the same time that milestone was reached, the company was sold to Sulzer and the original president resigned. The new president, Jerry Marlar, decided that the company needed a new vision that would take it to the next stage of development. He was also committed to a visioning process that would involve all the employees as well as external sales agents and other stakeholders.

The executive staff and one external sales agent met for four days to develop the first statement of the company's purpose, mission, values, and strategies for the year 2000. A month later 23 middle managers and two external sales agents met for three days to confirm, add to, and modify the work of the executive team. A third meeting merged both groups for four days to combine and integrate their work.

The results of the program (called Vision Quest 2000) were communicated to the entire staff in a series of one-hour meetings. After those preliminary announcement meetings, all employees and external sales agents were scheduled into 2 1/2 day Vision Quest sessions spread over a period of months.

Renee Rogers, the Training Coordinator and Organization Development Specialist at IOI, states the primary benefit of the shared visioning process, "By having everyone go through the process, we have developed a great deal more connection and commitment to the IOI objectives. There's also a much more sophisticated understanding of change and each person's role in IOI's future. The process of working backward from perfect to generate ideas and then using the CoNexus technology to find consensus really helped us separate the divergent thinking process from the convergent thinking stage."

Consensus Mapping

If restaurants were managed the way
many organizations are, the waiter would
tell you what to eat.
— from Leadership 2000 CoNexus brochure

The best idea generation in the world is useless if the ideas can't be implemented. When a new project or program is decided on, will it be carried out wholeheartedly or will a bunch of empty motions disguise the fact that the plan is being subverted? If the plan fails will it be because it was flawed or because it never had the necessary "buy-in?" There is an unlimited supply of excuses but they never add up to results.

In the early days of the Industrial Revolution, it was easy to tell when workers weren't working and they could be reprimanded, punished or fired if they weren't productive. In today's world of flex-time, telecommuting, outsourcing and decentralization, managers sometimes don't even see their "workers" and when they do see them, it's hard to determine what's "work" and what's not. Is that group huddled around the water fountain discussing a new way to lower costs or rehashing last night's football score? And if they are discussing football, is that a valuable part of building team comraderie or just goofing off? Is the person busily typing at the computer working on a report or playing Tetris? And, if she is playing Tetris, is that an important mental break that will add to her productivity or just a waste of time?

In the old days you could turn on a machine, tell the worker to shape up or ship out and you knew work would get done. Now when much of the "work" involves unseen mental processes, you can't force a person to work. But you can create an environment where work gets done well . . . and done exceedingly well . . . even when you aren't looking. For that to happen requires a high level of consensus on where you're going and how you're going to get there.

Building consensus into decision making processes can be as simple as verbally polling members of a team or as complicated as using keypad technology and software to provide statistical displays of the group opinions.

Graffiti Boards

One extremely simple, low-technology method of gathering opinions is the Graffiti Board. It can be used to sample opinions on anything from possible colors for the hallway to packaging for a new product. Giving people a chance to express their ideas and opinions is not only a good way to test the water on certain ideas, it heads off after-the-fact grumbling. When people have had a chance to express their opinions, they are much less likely to complain later, even if their preferred option was not the one selected. They feel listened to and have a chance to see, often for the first time, the wide variety of opinions that exist on almost any action.

For example, if you want to know what your staff thinks about a proposed new vacation policy or an organization change, you could put the question to a vote with a graffiti board. Post the question in a common area and provide Post-it™ notes for comments. If the question is a yes/no, you might want to create an intensity spectrum — "no" on the left, "yes" on the right. People who are less definite about their answers can post their votes toward the middle. Provide two colors of sticky notes (for example: yellow for "yes," blue for "no") for a visual tally of how the vote is running. Larger sticky notes also give people a place to write a short explanation of their vote or suggestions.

High Tech Tallying

At the other end of the complexity spectrum is

154

technology that rapidly collects group opinion in order to facilitate consensus. This technology is creating a revolution in meetings, planning and decision making as it quickly makes group opinions visible.

One example of this technology is CoNexus™, developed by Leadership 2000, which allows each member of the group to use a keypad to anonymously vote his or her choice in a forced-pair analysis of all the ideas generated. Each idea is compared to each of the others to determine preferences. Every member has an equal vote and the vote is private. The voting process is rapid but it requires the vote of each member of the group . . . the process does not continue until every person has voted. Thus full participation is insured regardless of group composition, politics or other group dynamics.

As soon as the voting is completed, the results are available for review and discussion. A map of the group's positions is immediately displayed and each person can recognize his or her position although there are no names attached to the position points. This gives the group a chance to review and discuss their degree of consensus on each voting item. Without this consensus map, the group might assume that a greater level of consensus exists because some opinions are not being vocalized. With the map, you can easily see the level of agreement or divergence.

If there are a few positions that are widely divergent from the group's, the facilitator can explore those points by asking: "What are some of the reasons someone might favor this position?" By encouraging the group to try to see outlying points of view, the entire group can discuss possibilities without getting into turf issues.

The following are the three primary causes of lack of consensus:

❐ Misunderstanding of terminology or meaning
❐ Uneven information base within the group
❐ True differences in points of view

Once the degree of divergence is mapped, each of these can be discussed. Terminology can be clarified, information can be shared and the basis for true differences can be explored. This process results in a much greater level of consensus and a clear statement of choices. At this point the group can decide whether they need more information in order to make a decision or whether they are ready to choose between the clarified positions. When a decision is made, there is a high level of group support which makes implementation of the decision much easier.

At Intermedics Orthopedics®, Inc., this consensus building technology proved so valuable that it was purchased for in-house use at the department and team level. Groups find that they can generate possibilities, map opinions, explore divergent opinions and achieve consensus in a much shorter time than they could with their previous methods.

Chapter Mindmap

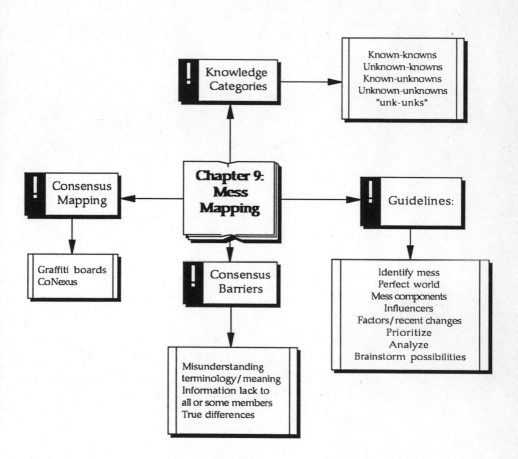

CHAPTER 10

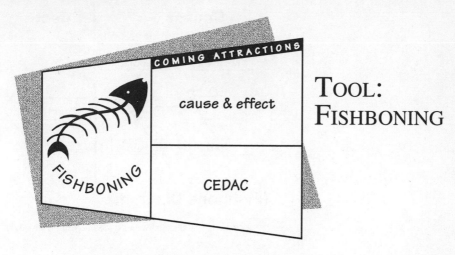

TOOL: FISHBONING

Tasks: Making things better

The unhealthiness of our world today is in direct proportion to our inability to see it as a whole.
— *Peter Senge,* **The Fifth Discipline**

Cause-and-effect diagrams were developed in 1943 by Kaoru Ishikawa at the University of Tokyo as a way to sort out various factors in a problem-solving process.

These diagrams graphically show the relationship between an effect (a problem) and its causes and have become one of the most commonly used Total Quality Management tools. They present an overview of the problem situation and hinder "one cause" thinking. Most imperfect situations have a variety of influences or causes and in order to make significant progress, all of the components of the system must be examined.

GOAL/QPC is a Massachusetts training organization that specializes in teaching Total Quality Management to organizations. They produce a pocket guide to tools for continuous improvement called *The Memory Jogger* which is used by 90 of the *Fortune 100* companies. This handy guide provides the following illustration and description of cause-and-effects diagrams and the steps in constructing them.

159

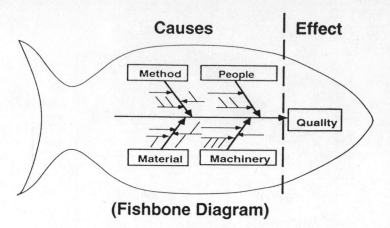

(Fishbone Diagram)

Reprinted with permission from GOAL/QPC

A well-detailed Cause & Effect Diagram will take on the shape of fishbones and hence the alternate name Fishbone Diagram. From this well-defined list of possible causes, the most likely are identified and selected for further analysis. When examining each cause, look for the things that have changed, deviations from the norm or patterns. Remember, look to cure the cause and not the symptoms of the problem. Push the causes back as much as is practically possible.

Steps in Constructing a Cause & Effect Diagram

1.) Generate the causes needed to build a Cause & Effect Diagram in one of two ways:
   - a.) Structured Brainstorming about possible causes without previous preparation.
   - b.) Ask members of the team to spend time between meetings using simple Check Sheets to track possible causes and to examine the production process steps closely.

2.) Construct the actual Cause & Effect Diagram by:
   - a.) Placing problem statement in box on the right.
   - b.) Drawing the traditional major cause category steps in the production process, or any causes that are helpful in organizing the most important factors.

160

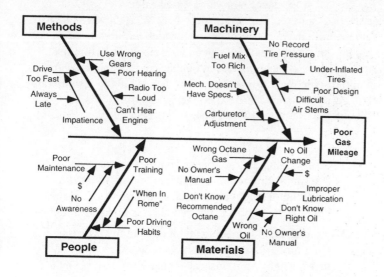

Reprinted with permission from GOAL/QPC

c.) Placing the Brainstormed ideas in the
appropriate major categories.
d.) For each cause ask, "Why does it happen?"
and list responses as branches off the major
causes.

3.) Interpretation. In order to find the most basic causes of
the problem:
a.) Look for causes that appear repeatedly.
b.) Reach a team consensus.
c.) Gather data to determine the relative
frequencies of the different causes.

CEDAC: Cause-and-Effect Diagrams and Cards

One limitation of cause-and-effect diagrams is the lack of
moveability of the information. Mine Safety Appliance (MSA) of
Pittsburgh, Pennsylvania, has developed a way to overcome that
limitation. Patricia Mettrick, training coordinator with MSA,
explains the CEDAC board, "It's basically a take-off on the cause-
and-effect diagram . . . the fishbone . . . that we learned from
Productivity, Inc. We use Post-it™ notes on the ribs so the
information can be moved around or changed."

MSA produces a broad range of safety devices — hardhats, respirators, etc. During the Gulf War, they won a bid with the military to make a gas mask which required bonding a urethane lens onto a molded silicon face piece. The complex bonding process was sensitive to bubbles and dust and resulted in an initial scrap rate of over 21 percent. MSA had bid a scrap rate of 10 percent so they were experiencing significant losses. Through the use of a CEDAC board, the scrap rate was reduced to 5.7 percent.

Process: Using a large sheet of paper, the cause-and-effect diagram is drawn on the right side of the sheet and graphing of actual data (a run chart) is posted on the far left side of the sheet. The run chart is updated weekly.

Participants: 8-10 people involved with the process, generally the frontline workers themselves — often facilitated by an industrial engineer, sometimes by a supervisor.

Topic: Chosen by the people involved. In the case of the gas mask, it was to reduce the scrap rate. Entered at the far right as the "effect."

Ribs: The group develops the ribs and brainstorms causes involved with each rib. Sometimes the ribs are the standard fishbone ribs (material, people, method, machinery) and sometimes the groups develop their own ribs such as tools, design, drawings, or engineering.

Causes: Once the ribs are selected, causes are listed on sticky notes and placed on the left side of the rib.

Solutions: Once all the causes are identified, possible solutions (usually at least 2-3 per cause) are generated and placed on the right side of the rib. For easy visual distinction of solutions from causes, a different color of sticky note is used for each.

Dotting: The group goes back over all the solutions and puts dots on all the solutions that seem to have potential. Once a solution is actually in process, another dot is added. The third dot is added later if the solution seems to be working. If a solution does not work out a line is drawn through the dots. If a three dot idea works out well, a box is drawn around it and it becomes a new standard.

At MSA most groups work with their CEDAC board for three or four months before redoing it. By that time it's usually necessary to redefine the problem, reassess the process or move on to a new problem. The gas mask problem was complex and the group working on it actually created three different boards before the scrap rate was reduced to 5.7 percent. People were brought in from different areas and shifts in order to generate new perspectives.

The CEDAC board is posted in a prominent place and anyone can add to it. "We ask them to sign and date their Post-it™ notes," states Mettrick, "so that we can get them to elaborate or explain their ideas if that is needed. But the board becomes a part of the brainstorming process as people add to it when ideas pop up."

In addition to the progress MSA made on the gas mask scrap rate, they reduced the price on a chemical canister from $8.10 to $5.30; reduced order entry time from 48 hours to 30 minutes; reduced machine set-up time from 5 hours to 25 minutes and reduced through-put from 5 days to 4 hours and saved 1100 square feet in one of their metals departments.

MSA's CEDAC board incorporates the four fundamentals of group thinking: it's participatory, information is presented visually and moveably, and the group has fun with the process, using killer balls, color and symbols to keep the sessions lighthearted.

FISHBONING

Chapter Mindmap

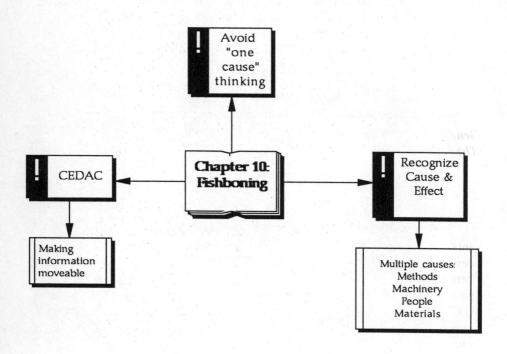

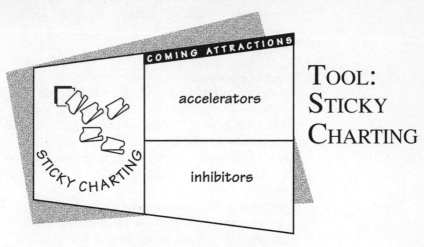

TOOL:
STICKY
CHARTING

Tasks: Making things better
         Communication

Generals don't win wars, and engineers don't build bridges.
The success of any endeavor depends entirely on those who
carry the plan to its ultimate fulfillment.
— General George Patton

W est Paces Ferry Hospital, a 294-bed hospital in
Atlanta was one of the first hospitals to implement a total quality
process. Like any organization that has diligently and honestly
concentrated on implementing a quality process, there is a
multitude of things they do right. However, one of the first things
CEO Chip Caldwell concentrated on was discovering what made
customers brag about the hospital. The next thing was to find out
how to make those brag-actions standard procedure — to do that
required a committed, motivated staff. Over years of working at
this process, West Paces developed a set of "accelerators and
inhibitors" — things that promote or hinder the kind of growth and
improvement they were seeking.

The accelerators they identified are:

❒ **meaningful work** — all members of the organization
    needed to understand how their efforts impacted patient
    care and the operations of the hospital.
❒ **vision** — there had to be a shared vision of excellence
    and quality patient care.

165

❐ **constant inquisitiveness** — the environment had to stimulate the belief that things could always be better.

The inhibitors they identified are:

❐ **lack of empowerment** — when people can't make independent judgments, they are forced to rely on written policies or supervisors. Both are inefficient in times of rapid change or in non-routine environments such as patient care in hospitals.

❐ **lack of structure** — when the structure isn't clear, people aren't sure what their roles are; what they should be doing and who their "customers" are.

❐ **impatience** — it takes time for people to learn new skills and gain mastery of them. Impatience or negative judgment during this learning period can cause an abandonment of effort. It becomes easier to do things the old way.

❐ **constantly changing policies** — people can adapt to change as long as the general direction remains the same. When the goals or policies change frequently, it creates a frustration in people who feel like they can never catch up.

❐ **failure to confront barriers** — every action has barriers which cannot be ignored or wished away. Management which "pooh-poohs" barriers trivializes the efforts involved with overcoming them. An honest identification of the barriers can lead to ideas for their successful elimination.

❐ **proceeding without evidence of readiness** — improvement programs of all types (total quality, customer service, creative problem solving) require new learning. Trying to force results from people who have not acquired sufficient understanding of mastery of the necessary skills, is an exercise in frustration.

❐ **unskilled facilitation** — facilitators, supervisors, and managers need the skills to guide the particular improvement process they are involved with. They need to recognize blocks, understand when additional training is needed, identify communication barriers, resolve conflicts and keep the group focused on the goals. Too many organizations assume that all of these skills come packaged with the first promotion to supervisor.

STICKY CHARTING

Sticky Charting

West Paces does a lot of visual thinking. They tend to describe everything visually, using cause-and-effect diagrams, mindmaps, storyboards and process symbols. It was at West Paces that we first saw flow charting done with Post-it™ notes . . . they called it sticky charting. Different colored Post-it™ notes were used for various processes, or in some cases the sticky notes were turned a different direction to indicate specific processes or actions. Because anyone can diagram a process using Post-it™ notes, a highly sophisticated thinking tool was made accessible to everyone in the organization.

West Paces also uses this concept for their new product development process. They have a flow chart of all the steps required to effectively design, test, release and market a new product. When a new product is decided on, they put the product name on a Post-it™ note and stick it to the beginning of the flow chart. As the product flows through the process, its progress is tracked on the flow chart. It is an instant visual status sheet for all products and provides a mechanism for recognizing when certain products have bogged down or developed problems.

"Something unexpected happened . . . "

Another example of sticky charting comes from Grumman Technical Services where Mark Morgan is the manager of the Total Quality Management program. His group wanted to illustrate the organization's processes for the senior review team so they did a sticky chart . . . what they called a process tree. They began by identifying the major operations and processes — business services (accounting, payroll, etc.), technical services (calibration, repair of equipment and systems, etc.). Work teams then began breaking the processes down into sub levels and processes. Morgan explains, "Everything we did as an organization was illustrated on this 10' x 6' diagram — 850 individual tasks were linked together in this chart.

"Something unexpected happened when it was all laid out. We posted the diagram in an active conference room — almost everyone came through the room in the course of the week for one meeting or another. We found people stopping to look at the chart and understand it — they would look for their place on the chart and say, 'Wow, that's what I do — I never really understood how I fit into the whole process.' They gained insight as to their individual role.

"People began to leave notes to correct language and processes. They got involved with the process map and when the steering committee began to look for improvements, they had a picture of the entire operation. They could begin to see how changes would ripple through the entire operation.

"Prior to that we would charter a team to go look at a piece of the system and they would feel disconnected. When we talked about doing something that impacted profit, they would say, 'We aren't involved with profit.' or 'What we do doesn't impact that.' By using this diagram, we could show their connection to cost measures or defect measures that then related to profit.

"Our overhead rates have come down by 18% which helped us win a $340 million job. All of our 12 key indicators have shown steady improvements. Our accounting team's ability to report information improved significantly. They consolidated several processes and had an 88% improvement in the cycle time for producing financial reports. This also allowed them to cut staff by five people ... from a total staff of 15."

"Something unexpected happened," is a frequent comment that occurs when groups of people can look at and think about an entire process. Suddenly they see inefficiences and new possibilities. They recognize their place in the scheme of things and begin to feel more of a sense of impact and ownership.

Sticky Charting Process:

❐ **Assemble the right people.** Make sure a cross-section of people are involved and that they represent all aspects of the process.

❐ **Describe the process** to be charted, setting the beginning point and ending point. A typical order entry process would begin when an order was received from a customer and end when the order was transmitted to the product fulfillment area and accounting.

❐ **Determine the major steps.** Break the process down into its major components. In the order entry example, the major steps might be sorting, computer entry, cash/credit card processing, credit verification, exception handling and storage. Each major step is represented by a larger sticky note on the left side of the chart paper.

❐ **Identify detail steps.** Look at each major step and ask, "What's the first thing that happens?" That step is represented by a Post-it™ placed next to the major step. The next step is identified and placed next to the previous note. Decision points can be represented by turning the note so that it is a diamond rather than a rectangle. Each path of the decision point is developed to its conclusion before continuing with the mainstream of the process.

❐ **Differentiate departments or locations.** Different colored Post-it™ notes can be used to represent different departments or locations. This can help visually show interaction between departments or movement of the product or process.

❐ **Display the chart.** Display the chart where others can see it and invite them to add their comments, but not to change the existing chart. Provide a supply of Post-it™ notes so their comments can be easily added or moved. Periodically the original group can meet and process the added comments, adjusting the chart as needed.

Sticky charting is a powerful tool for visually displaying processes and helping people understand their role in the process. Just the process of developing the chart often reveals inefficiencies and opportunities. Comments such as *I never did understand why we did it that way . . . Someone asked for that report several years ago and we've been doing it ever since . . . We get all this information and we don't do anything with it . . .* and *Isn't there an easier way?* are heard frequently during the process as age-old habits and redundant procedures come to light.

Chapter Mindmap

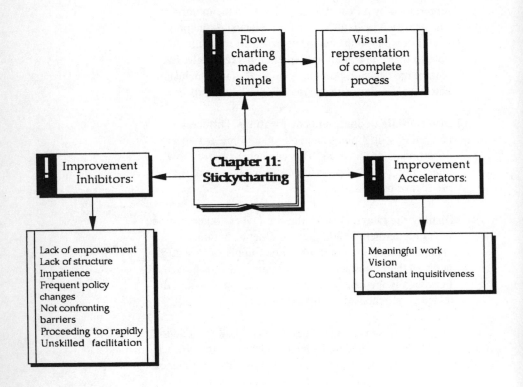

Flow charting made simple

Visual representation of complete process

Chapter 11: Stickycharting

Improvement Inhibitors:

Improvement Accelerators:

Lack of empowerment
Lack of structure
Impatience
Frequent policy
changes
Not confronting
barriers
Proceeding too rapidly
Unskilled facilitation

Meaningful work
Vision
Constant inquisitiveness

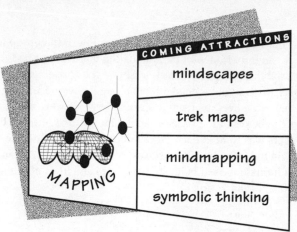

CHAPTER 12

TOOL:
MINDMAPS
TO
MINDSCAPES

*Special thanks to Nancy Margulies for contributing this chapter. Nancy is a gifted consultant, corporate mindmapping facilitator, artist, and author of **Mapping Inner Space** and the video, **Maps, Mindscapes & More.***

Tasks: Making things better
              Making leaps
              Project management
              Training
              Communication

In La Port, Texas, the DuPont plant houses four divisions and management recognized the need for the divisions to stay in touch with each other and work together to achieve their shared objectives. They wanted the divisions to recognize that they had many issues in common . . . such as safety and quality . . . as well as their beliefs and values. I was invited to help them brainstorm ways to develop, visually represent, and communicate a shared vision. In searching for a visual metaphor, we considered an underwater treasure hunt, a trip through outer space, a hike through the woods and running along a race track.

We selected a mountain-climbing trek where the group vision was represented inside a billowing cloud at the top of the mountain. Empowered individuals were represented by four mountain climbers (one for each division) climbing separately but connected by safety ropes. None of the climbers could go too far beyond the group and they needed to stay aware and thoughtful about the positions of the others. Only together could they reach their goal.

Further developing the metaphor allowed the group to recognize the importance of the foundation that DuPont had already established and to identify many of the barriers and milestones that might be encountered along the way. Limiting beliefs that often keep us from reaching our goals were represented by people in boxes at the base of the mountain. One of the tasks of the climbers was to help each other out of those boxes before they could begin the journey. These boxes, or initial barriers, often represent limits imposed by customary roles and lines of authority in traditional organizations.

MAPPING

Mindscapes: Mapping the Organization's Journey

There is a burgeoning need among corporate leaders to "see the big picture" and be "visionary." Mindmapping, one of the most popular systems for recording ideas, speaks to the too-often-inactive right hemisphere in a visual, spatial language. On a neurological level, color and images activate the right hemisphere of the cerebral cortex and create a more whole-brain thinking environment. Once business people understand the fundamental reasons for mapping, they are eager to pick up their colored pens and begin representing their ideas symbolically.

However, the visual map DuPont created was different from the mindmapping process (which we will describe in detail later) used in corporations and schools across the U.S. and in countries around the world. While mindmapping is a powerful thinking tool, DuPont's visual metaphor of its journey required going beyond mindmapping. We needed a new term for this process and I decided on the term "Mindscape." Mindscapes are a less structured, "no rules," graphic approach to looking at the context as well as the details of any given topic. The free form structure allows new ideas to be added wherever they fit within the over-all picture.

Mindscapes encourage us to find visual metaphors for our situations — goals can be shown at the end of a road or in clouds overhead. We can depict roadblocks, possible dead ends, bridges, sidetracks, and other challenges of journeying toward a goal. A visual image of the journey creates images which are much more vivid and engaging than a words-only description.

For the DuPont group, I created a mural-sized Mindscape poster of the organization's trek which was then displayed in the plant so that everyone could see where they were going and what they had already accomplished, all on one sheet of paper. It helped them remember that everyone was climbing in the same basic direction toward a shared goal.

MAPPING

"Trek Mindscapes"

One of DuPont's objectives was to have every individual participate and understand this process, so we created an individual Mindscape exercise. Each person was given a small Mindscape of the mountain trek and instructed to think of a time when they had successfully completed a project or achieved a goal. Each person symbolized a goal in the cloud and then depicted the resources used on the trek, the milestones and markers along the way, and what boulders had to be pushed out of the way to achieve the goal. This "Trek Mindscape" helped them acknowledge successes in their lives, identifying the types of resources they used and the barriers they overcame.

If you decide to do a Mindscape, be bold! You might want to use a sheet of paper that takes up an entire wall (supply stores have 3' x 8' rolls of white paper that work well for Mindscaping). Begin wherever you wish; draw your own pictures or use some from magazines. While mindmapping begins with a central image, it is not necessary in a Mindscape. Sometimes you may want to make a large image on the page and fill it in with your notes, ideas and symbols. You might write an idea on each half of the paper and compare or contrast the two across the page or make a large image and fill it with notes, ideas and symbols. You could also make a Mindscape that resembles a jigsaw puzzle, a board game or a racetrack.

Use whatever resources are on hand. Post-it™ notes are good for adding new ideas and moving them around the Mindscape to reflect new possibilities or conditions. Provide everyone with a supply of different colored Post-it™ notes and encourage them to add ideas wherever they seem to fit.

When using Mindscaping to capture the thoughts of a group, challenge yourselves. Ask provocative questions such as:

> *How can we visually describe our goals?*
> *What metaphors might describe how we work together?*
> *How would we like to see ourselves?*
> *What is the environment we are trying to create?*
> *What are some possible scenes from our future?*

MAPPING

Another example of mindscaping comes from MEMC's St. Peters, Missouri, plant which manufacturers silicon wafers. The plant's top management decided that their vision was for each person to receive a return on his or her investment, whether that involved time, energy, relationships or capital. We called this concept RFI (return from investment) and created a personal mindmap that helped each person answer the questions "What do I put into my job?" and "What do I want to get out of it?" A similar mindmap encouraged customers, suppliers and even stockholders to examine their personal RFIs and to share the results with MEMC/St. Peters. These individual mindmaps helped people think much more broadly about their situation rather than focusing narrowly on paychecks or benefits. Composite Mindscapes of RFIs were posted for everyone to see. The following is an employee RFI:

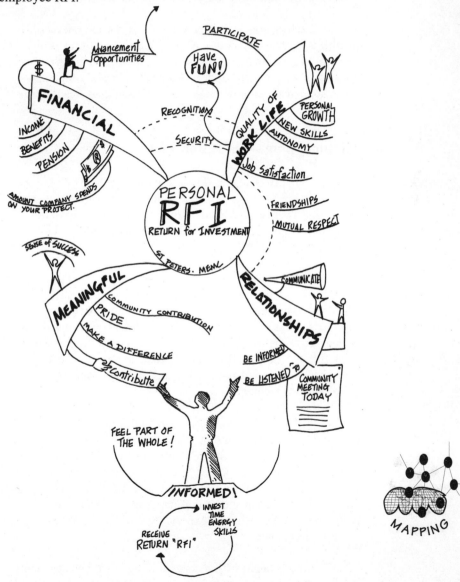

We found that people appreciated the opportunity to create their personal RFI maps as a way to clarify their thinking and share their ideas with others. Once each segment had mapped its personal RFI, we began to build these individual visions into a Mindscape mural which represented MEMC's shared vision. Beginning with RFI in the center, concentric circle representing values, mission and strategic goals ripple like water in a pond.

Each person looking at the RFI Mindscape can consider whether a specific decision or action leads toward the central vision or away from it. The Mindscape provides a blueprint for decision-making which supports MEMC/St. Peters' on-going efforts to increase empowerment and value-centered leadership.

Mindmapping — Is It For You?

Mindmapping is a simple skill that can help you see the big picture, capture complex ideas quickly and easily and identify relationships between ideas and processes. Once you have the basics of mindmapping under your belt, you can move on to Mindscaping.

Using pictures to convey ideas is natural to all of us. Remember your own childhood when you drew freely — happily conveying your ideas in ways that were meaningful to you? The early beginnings of mindmapping can be found on cave walls and ancient scrolls on which hieroglyphics display ideas symbolically. Tony Buzan, who coined and popularized the term in the late 60s, extensively researched and documented the effectiveness of this visual thinking technique.

MAPPING

Mindmapping is easy to learn and, with a little practice, easy to use. Unlike the outlining we learned in school, mindmapping organizes information in a non-linear, colorful, symbolic fashion. Also, unlike outlining, mindmapping allows you great freedom! It's a very natural way of using your mind. Just as all minds are different, each mindmap is unique. Here are a few guidelines that will help you experience the benefits of this powerful technique:

❏ **always begin with a central image** — if you absolutely cannot find a symbolic way to represent the focus of your thinking, print a representative word in a central circle, cloud, or other shape in the middle of the page.

❐ **print one key word per line** — the brain recognizes patterns and needs only a tiny bit of information to trigger a complex pattern.

❐ **all lines branch from the central image** — lines help us make links and associations among various pieces of information.

Although symbols and pictures are not mandatory, you will discover that the more you use colors and symbols, the more memorable your maps will be and the more you will stimulate your visual thinking abilities.

When brainstorming alone or with a group, you can map all of your ideas on a single sheet of paper. Instead of listing all the ideas in the order they are generated, mindmapping allows you to group them by topic, show connections between ideas and highlight lines of influence.

Symbolic Thinking

Mindmaps can be complex or simple and can vary from primarily words to 100% pictures. The process of using mindmapping helps us develop our ability to think visually and symbolically. Look around you — symbols are everywhere. From signs in airports to icons on computer screens — we increasingly communicate not only in words, but with images.

Mindmap Activity I

Try your first mindmap right now! Grab a pen and paper: it's best if the paper is unlined, but if it's ruled, just turn the paper sideways and ignore the lines. In the center of the page, draw a symbol that represents this book. (Don't worry about your drawing skills! The reason for drawing is to turn on the part of your brain that uses symbolic language . . . not to demonstrate your artistic talent.)

MAPPING

From that central image, draw a line that curves slightly and, on that line, print a word that represents one of the topics of this book. If you have further thoughts about that topic, branch from the original line and print additional key words as they occur to you. The following is a skeleton map to show how the lines might branch from a central image:

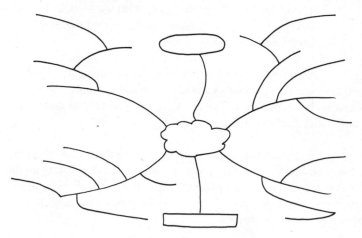

Although most adults believe that they can't draw, the fact is that everyone can, if they are open to trying and willing to practice. My hope is that schools of the future will teach drawing — not as an act of art . . . but as a communication skill. In order to open your mind to the possibility that YOU can communicate symbolically, copy the following symbols on a separate sheet of paper. Begin to build your own symbolic vocabulary. Once you are comfortable drawing a basic set of symbols, you will be able to use them to convey ideas to others.

MAPPING

When you study these symbols, you can see that they are much less complex than the printed words associated with them. Yet for most of us, writing has become such a habit that we think printing a word such as L-E-T-T-E-R is easier than drawing:

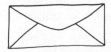

Drawing an envelope is easy, once you have tried it a time or two. Indicating that the letter needs to go out right away can be accomplished by adding lines or wings. Not only is the envelope easy to draw, but it is easy to "read" at a glance and more memorable than the printed word.

Mindmap Activity II

Time to do a mindmap about a topic of your choice. Use colored pens and unlined paper (large-sized computer paper is great and easel pads give you lots of room to think BIG). Turn the paper sideways (on the horizontal) and think of a topic. I suggest that you map a project you're involved in, or are planning to initiate. In the center of the paper, draw a symbol of the project. Make it meaningful to you. Any image will automatically produce two results: it will be more memorable and it will engage the imaginative, pattern-making right hemisphere of your brain.

Colors also appeal to the right hemisphere, so use several. Later you may want to use color as a way to organize your ideas . . . for now, just make your map colorful. Let ideas occur to you without concern as to which are important and which aren't. Record them all — even the far-fetched ones. Each idea is represented by a single word or image on a line, radiating from the central image. When you have thoughts related to a key word, continue to branch out from that word. The branches will begin to grow like limbs on a tree. An idea that represents a new topic is placed on a new line, connected to the central image. Finding key words may initially be a challenge, but it will help refine and clarify your thinking.

You can emphasize ideas or concepts by making a word larger, varying the lettering style, underlining or circling the word or highlighting it with color. You are free to create your own "new grammar" of color, shape, size and location on the page. These extra dimensions will make the notes more memorable also.

MAPPING

When working with corporate developers of instructional design, I ask everyone to make a mindmap of a time they remember enjoying the learning process. The following is a quick map I created to record all the feelings, motivations and rewards I associate with learning to roller-skate.

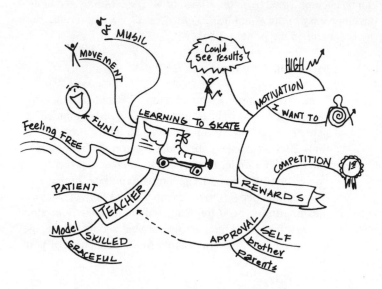

Try mindmapping your most rewarding learning experience. These "learning maps" can be used to generate ideas about how to recreate that excitement and enthusiasm in a training session or other learning situations. This type of mapping stretches us to think outside our usual paradigms.

Your mindmaps will look completely different from mine (and from everyone else's). There is no wrong way to do it, as long as your map reflects the information and connections that have meaning for you.

Electronic Data Systems (EDS) has taught mindmapping to approximately 6,000 members of it's organization. One project leader liked his group's mindmap so much that he had a graphic artist make it more visually appealing. He then distributed color copies to everyone on the team. The title of the map is "Take Advantage of Change" and many people framed it and still have it hanging in their offices. On the back of the map is an in-depth explanation of the map and the project. Although their change map is too complex and colorful to be reproduced in this space, it represents a complex, sophisticated approach to change that continues to motivate the team and others in the organization.

Personal "Trek Mindscape"

If you would like to do your own "Trek Mindscape" like the one created by the team at DuPont, here's how:

❏ First, copy the following simplified version of the mountain and cloud illustration on a sheet of paper that is at least 11" x 17."*

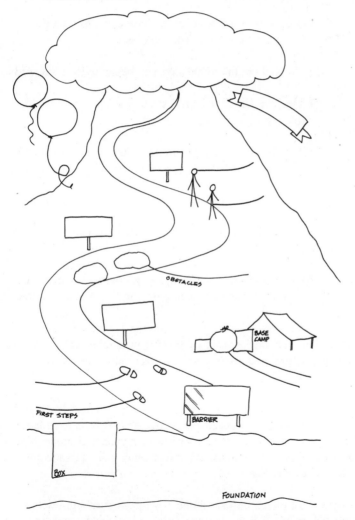

*If you would like a free supply of pre-printed "treks," call 1-800-200-0919

❒ Think of a successful experience that was especially rewarding. Fill in the cloud with an image or key word description of the goal you achieved.

❒ Recall the process you went through to obtain the goal. Think about the limits you had to overcome. Represent them in the box and barrier pictured at the bottom of the page.

❒ Use the bag and boxes at the base camp to record resources or supplies you needed.

❒ Think about the foundation you began with and record it.

❒ Describe the first steps that you took in key words or images.

❒ Record obstacles in the boulder shape on the road and add a word or image that shows how you overcame them.

❒ Fill in the sign posts (accomplishments) along the road.

❒ Use the balloons to record celebrations, recognitions, or rewards.

❒ Who accompanied, assisted or encouraged you in this project? Write their names next to the fellow travelers on the road.

❒ If you were guided by specific principles, values, or a role model, record that in the banner below the cloud.

MAPPING

Producing a visual "Trek Mindscape" is an excellent way to acknowledge yourself or your team for a job well-done. It also helps you know how to use the information gained to accomplish your next objective.

To plan a project (alone or with a team) begin with a blank Trek Mindscape. Use the space in the cloud to record your "vision" or goal. This could be a short-term personal or professional project, or a long-range plan.

Think about anything that might limit you — these can be beliefs, habits, or systems. Label the limiting boxes and barriers. Decide how you can "get out of your box" in order to journey to the mountain top.

Continue to add to the map as you develop your plan. If you are planning with a group, each person can make an individual Trek Mindscape. Discuss the various elements of your maps, then collaborate to create a final map reflecting the team plan.

The signposts along the road can be used to record actions or as benchmarks of certain achievements. These also help underscore that a variety of projects or initiatives are not necessarily unrelated . . . not the "flavor of the month" . . . but are part of one journey.

If you encounter a boulder in the road, label it and create a plan for moving beyond it, or finding an alternative path.

Post the Trek Mindscape where you can see it and check your progress regularly. Plan a celebration or reward when you reach a certain point on the journey. Be sure to measure success in more than one way. For example, although success might be a certain profit, volume or quota, it might also involve learning, building team spirit or improving communication.

When your trek map is complete, study it, asking yourself the following questions:

What are the limits or barriers to overcome in order to take the trek?
What provisions will I need?
Who will support me?
What do I contribute to the journey?
Where am I (or Where are we) on the path right now?
Which sign posts would be most meaningful to me?
Which barriers are boulders that must be removed?
How will we measure and celebrate success?

Mindmapping and Mindscaping Applications

MAPPING

The applications for Mindscapes and mindmaps are quite diverse. Margaret Wheatley, author of the breakthrough management book, *Leadership and the New Science* is one of the initiators of a dialogue group that meets regularly in Utah to discuss applications of the new science. I create Mindscapes to capture the ideas and questions that emerge during these meetings. The following Mindscape was created to help participants remember and share new ideas:

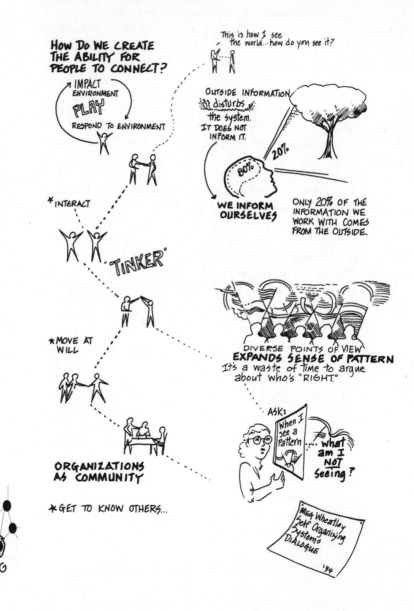

Because mindmapping and mindscaping help make information more memorable and allow people to incorporate their own associations and linkages, it is an excellent tool for teachers and trainers. During training courses or seminars, a great deal of information is presented. Many seminars give participants a special mapping journal for recording their ideas and thoughts. At the end of each session they encourage participants to spend a few minutes to reflect on the lessons of that session.

Michael W. Munn, Ph.D., Director of Creativity for Lockheed Missiles & Space Company, Inc., divides his training sessions into 90-minute segments followed by a break. Students spend the last five minutes of each segment mapping their thoughts and ideas. When they return from break, they take five minutes to share their thoughts with another participant. This reinforces their learning in several ways: they recapture their thoughts through the mapping process, refine and clarify their thoughts by explaining them to someone else and acquire other interpretations and associations by listening to another person's thoughts on the same material.

Mindmapping or mindscaping can also rescue complex negotiations. Imagine a business meeting, a counseling session or a classroom. The persons who need to reach an agreement are asked to select a few colored markers and each draw a symbol in the center of a large sheet of paper. Each person's symbol/key word represents his or her personal notion of the ideal outcome of this negotiation.

Next, each person is asked to branch out from the central image, recording in blue all the elements of this ideal outcome. Using a new color, each person then adds specifics to each branch about what he or she would be willing to do to create each aspect of that desired outcome.

People are then paired and instructed: "Walk your partner through your map. Explain your thoughts. Then listen while your partner does the same." These partners are two people from "opposite" sides of the negotiation. They are then asked to make one map, working together to record all the areas on which they agree. They then add to the map what each would do in order to further any of their shared goals. At this point the seemingly opposing sides have worked as partners and are now ready to begin talking about areas in which agreement must still be

MAPPING

negotiated. In large groups, each "couple" joins with another "couple" and create a map of shared ideas for the four-some. This could continue until there was one large map for the entire group.

Tips

Mindmaps and Mindscapes are most often used in addition to other forms of communication. Rarely do they need to stand alone. Most of the maps you make will be a record for your own reference, or to remind others of a discussion or presentation. The maps in this chapter will convey ideas to you, but they should be read with the understanding that a written or verbal explanation may be needed to provide additional details.

When mapping, print words so that you can read them without turning or tipping the paper. To accomplish this, curve the lines slightly or put the words in boxes as shown in previous maps:

Whenever you draw a symbol ask yourself if the meaning will be clear to you in a week or a month. If the answer is "no," add a key word. If you want to learn more about mindmapping and Mindscapes, here are some excellent additional reading materials:

❑ *Mindmapping: Your Personal Guide to Exploring Creativity and Problem-Solving* by Joyce Wycoff (Berkley Publishing Group, 1991).
An excellent guide to the basics of mindmapping and many of its uses.

❑ *Mapping Inner Space* by Nancy Margulies (Zephyr Press, 1991).
A fun, creative guide to mindmapping with emphasis on creating symbols and images. Also shows you how to help students use this powerful learning tool. The book includes one sample map for every page of text.

MAPPING

❑ *Maps, Mindscapes and More* by Nancy Margulies.
A how-to video for teachers on the uses of mapping and Mindscapes in the classroom.

❑ *Map-It! A Comic Book Approach to Mapping for Teens* by Nancy Margulies

Mapping: The Conclusion

Mapping isn't the answer to every challenge, but it is an excellent tool for enhancing your thinking and communication skills. At the very least, mindmapping provides a method for rapidly recording ideas. At the most, it can open up a whole new career path . . . as it did for me. I use mapping to assist my clients in every task from strategic planning to communicating with foreign partners. During the past ten years, I have mapped legal defenses, resumes, life plans, organizational transitions, grocery lists, ideas for Halloween costumes and helped my children map their homework and study for tests with Mindscapes. I also created Mindscapes while working with The President and Cabinet of the United States, helped clients introduce new employees, Mindscaped the entire system of an international office supply business, mapped the details for editing a motion picture, and Mindscaped plans for a nationwide education system for the country of Liechtenstein.

As another example, here's a Mindscape that was created while I worked with the USDA during their 1994 Senior Policy Retreat.

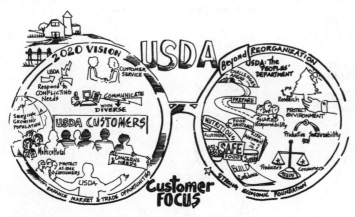

Mindmapping and mindscaping are powerful devices for organizing information, generating ideas, communicating with other people, solving problems and creating a learning and thinking environment. I truly believe that large sheets of paper and colored markers are just as important and as effective in boardrooms as are graphs, flowcharts and traditional written and verbal reports.

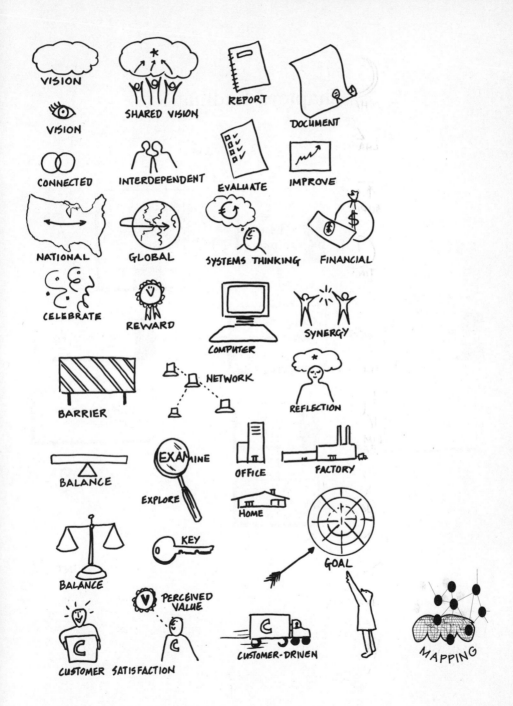

Chapter Mindmap

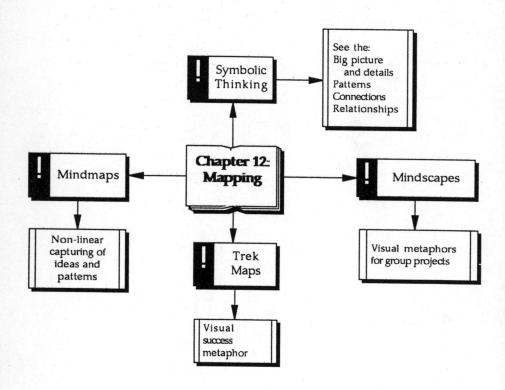

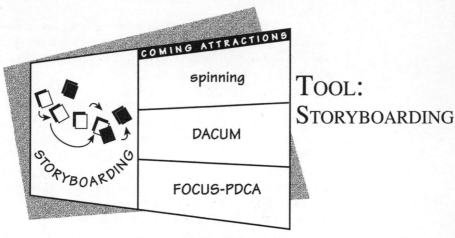

Tasks: Making things better
Making leaps
Concordant decision making
Project management
Training
Communication

When inspiration does not come to me,
I go halfway to meet it.
— Sigmund Freud

Storyboarding is a versatile tool that seems to be "owned" by three separate groups of users: advertising/art layout folks, total quality management people, and idea generators. Advertising and film people storyboard their work in order to document the flow and the interaction of visuals and text. Total quality management people use a specific storyboard layout to document an improvement process and serve as a communication mechanism for the improvement team and others within the organization. The primary use we're interested in is storyboarding for idea generation and problem solving.

One well-known storyboard trainer is Jerry McNellis who was introduced to the storyboarding process at the Walt Disney Studios where it was used for planning animated cartoons. McNellis calls his storyboard process "compression planning" because it produces innovative results rapidly by blending collaborative leadership concepts with visual group processes. It results in an open, creative planning session which stimulates the thinking process while maintaining structure and organization.

"Squeezing time out of group projects requires a team of key people determined to resolve their issue within hours or days, not weeks or months," states McNellis. "High speed collaboration and decisive action are demanded.

"For instance, I recently facilitated a sales conference of about 250 people. The sales people had historically moaned and groaned about the break-out sessions so we changed the process and broke them out into about twenty storyboarding groups. Each group took the company's key strategy for the coming year and worked on how to implement it. They met for one morning and generated ideas. That night we took over a Kinko's and reproduced reports which were presented the next morning. The rest of the conference was spent designing action plans. They were blown away by the process and what they accomplished in such a short time.

"We spend a lot of time on up-front design and helping people write header cards. If you ask good questions, you tend to get better answers. Writing a topic or header card may take 20 rewrites. *What is the issue? What are we really about? What's the critical background people need to know?* It's also critical to communicate the pivotal background participants need to effectively participate in the planning process. Thinking through what people need to know to participate helps leaders and facilitators understand all the issues involved with the situation.

Spinning Ideas

McNellis continues, "We've also moved away from the standard brainstorming idea of putting one idea on a card. We do something called "spinning" — it includes more words per card resulting in fewer cards but more complete ideas. We try to get an actionable idea on each card and have found that our progress is much more significant. It seems like the major compression of time comes when people generate complete thoughts. We hold the group on one idea until it is congealed enough to be action-able, prototype-able and cost-able. We call it breaking the brainstorming habit.

"We don't judge the merits of the idea but we keep forming and refining the idea until it meets the three criteria of being action-able, prototype-able and cost-able. We are not saying it's good or bad, but we are saying it's formed or not formed. Then, when you go to the evaluation stage, you have something to evaluate.

"One example that occurs in almost all planning or problem solving sessions is that someone says, 'We need to improve communication.' We wouldn't put that on the board. We would work with it and say, 'Let's build on that idea.' If someone said, 'We need to tie everyone together with e-mail,' that would fit the criteria of being action-able, cost-able or prototype-able. We try to teach people to think in action ideas and prototypes, then you have a totally different type of thought happening."

As a further example of how McNellis forces a group into actionable ideas, if they were brainstorming problems in a manufacturing environment, people would generally throw out problem ideas such as "bearings" or "grease." In a standard brainstorming process, the group would fill sheets with the problem ideas and then have to go back and take each idea and try to come up with specifics. In the McNellis method, the process might go something like this:

Group:	Bearings.
Facilitator:	What about the bearings?
Group:	We don't have conformance.
Facilitator:	Conformance with what?
Group:	We've got all kinds of different sizes.
Facilitator:	What could we do about that?
Group:	We need to get down to just a few sizes that would fit everything.
Facilitator:	What would be an example of that?
Group:	We need about a dozen sizes that would fit in every situation.

In order to generate more than one idea, the facilitator can ask, "What else could you do to gain conformance?" This "actionable" idea approach can yield a quantity of solid ideas. However, it may not uncover radically new ideas. If you are trying to develop new products or make leaps into totally new ways of thinking, you may want to try one of the other thinking tools or use some of the idea stimulators discussed in Chapter 4 to loosen up the thought process prior to using the McNellis approach.

The "Spastic Lurch"

McNellis was doing a training workshop in Texas when a participant approached him and he asked her how she was doing. The woman replied, "You know, we were into continuous improvement and then the chairman came along and said that wasn't good enough — we needed to start making quantum leaps and shifting our paradigms. We keep trying to do all these things but the best we seem to do is every once in a while we have a good spastic lurch."

The woman was obviously a victim of a management-by-quick-fix mentality but McNellis observes: *If we can help people "spastically lurch" somewhat together, maybe that's as much progress as we can expect.*

DACUM — Job Analysis

Margaret Downey, a trainer with CSX Transportation, uses a variation of storyboarding known as DACUM (Developing A Curriculum) to analyze occupations, breaking them down into specific tasks. The DACUM charts can be used to develop job descriptions and evaluation criteria, design training programs, develop competency tests, or use as part of the recruitment process. The DACUM process operates on three basic assumptions:

❑ Expert workers are the best source for task analysis.
❑ Any occupation can be effectively described in terms of tasks.
❑ All tasks imply knowledge, skills, and attitudes or values.

Generally, DACUM charts are developed during a two-day, facilitated process by 8-10 experts in the occupational area being charted. The DACUM profile generated during this process is a detailed and graphic portrayal of the skills or competencies involved in the occupation. The final chart lists tasks down the left side of the sheet and sequenced steps posted horizontally to the right.

STORYBOARDING

Storyboarding Legal Cases

Ed Preston is the president of Ed Preston & Associates, a planning facilitation group in Jacksonville, Florida, that works predominantly with attorneys on major cases. Preston studied with Jerry McNellis and now facilitates three- to four-hour sessions for his clients to help them gain a new perspective on and insights into the complex tangle of evidence, testimony, legal strategies and damage claims of the case. He combines the storyboarding technique with a focus group format that also helps the attorneys understand how people respond to the facts and evidence of the case.

Storyboarding is part of the creative thinking process that "generates, provokes, explores, entertains and fantasizes," states Preston. "The smallest building blocks of storyboards are ideas. The simplest form of an idea contains a noun and a verb."

Preston's clients gather 6-8 people together for the storyboarding session. The group generally includes some people who are familiar with the case or a similar case, some who have no familiarity with it and at least one devil's advocate. Preston states, "The most common statement I hear at the end of a session is, 'I would never have dreamed that this aspect of the case would be that important.'"

Preston works with his clients to develop 4-5 topics which are placed at the top of each storyboard. 6-8 header cards are then pinned just below the topic card.

Participants are given the following ground rules:

- ❐ suspend judgment — no negatives
- ❐ be freewheeling
- ❐ quantity is the aim
- ❐ cheat off your neighbor — piggyback on his ideas
- ❐ comments must be limited to 15 seconds

Anyone who uses a killer phrase or breaks a ground rule is hit with "killer balls" — nerf balls that are given to each participant. "Lawyers are such analytical thinkers, they always get hit with the killer balls," Preston states.

Participants generate ideas, writing them down on their index cards and relaying them to the group. As the facilitator or an assistant pins the idea card to the board, the facilitator repeats the ideas to help stimulate further ideas in the group.

> EXAMPLE: MEDICAL MALPRACTICE CASE
>
> **Sample Board Topic Card:**
> Liability
> **Sample Header Card:**
> What did the doctor do wrong?
> **Sample Idea Cards:**
> Didn't follow proper procedure
> Incorrect diagnosis
> Prescribed inappropriate medication

Concensus Dotting: Once the idea-generation cycle is completed, the participants go through a "consensus dotting" process. Each person can spend three dots in each header category, either voting for the three ideas he thinks are most important or spending all his dots on one idea if he thinks it far outranks the others.

The cards are removed in order of the voting and reproduced on 8 1/2 by 14 sheets laid out to represent the storyboards.

Storyboard Process:

❏ **Form group** — Pick 6-9 participants with a broad mix of backgrounds who have an interest in the project.

❏ **Explain process and ground rules** — Make sure people understand the difference between the idea generation process and the evaluation process. Give each participant a stack of cards and a thick felt-tipped marker. Explain how to make notes with key words — nouns, verbs and critical descriptors only. Give them killer balls to attack killer phrases.

❏ **Explain the basics of the project** — Give the participants enough information to basically understand the situation and start generating ideas. Be careful not to bias the group or lead them.

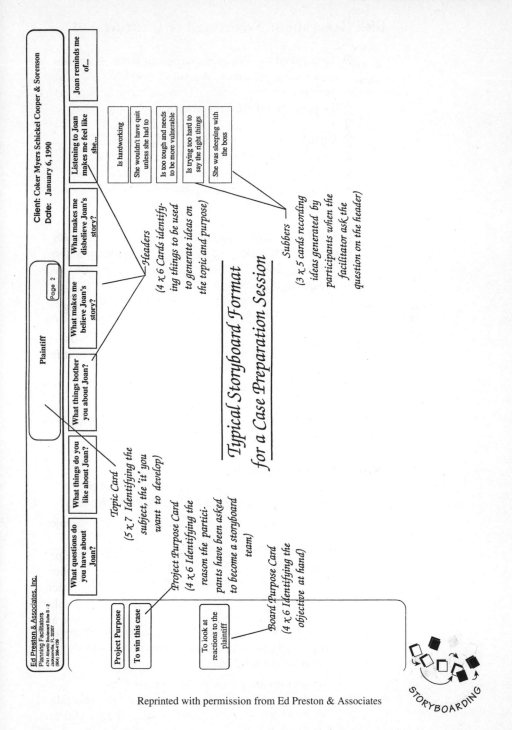

Ed Preston & Associates, Inc.
Planning Facilitators
4741 Atlantic Boulevard Suite B - 2
Jacksonville, FL 32207
(904) 396-4139

Client: Coker Myers Schickel Cooper & Sorenson
Date: January 6, 1990

Plaintiff   Page 2

| What questions do you have about Joan? | What things do you like about Joan? | What things bother you about Joan? | What makes me believe Joan's story? | What makes me disbelieve Joan's story? | Listening to Joan makes me feel like she... | Joan reminds me of... |

Topic Card
(5 x 7 Identifying the subject, the 'it' you want to develop)

Headers
(4 x 6 Cards identifying things to be used to generate ideas on the topic and purpose)

Is hardworking

She wouldn't have quit unless she had to

Is too tough and needs to be more vulnerable

Is trying too hard to say the right things

She was sleeping with the boss

Subbers
(3 x 5 cards recording ideas generated by participants when the facilitator ask the question on the header)

Project Purpose Card
(4 x 6 Identifying the reason the participants have been asked to become a storyboard team)

Project Purpose

To win this case

To look at reactions to the plaintiff

Board Purpose Card
(4 x 6 Identifying the objective at hand)

Typical Storyboard Format
for a Case Preparation Session

STORYBOARDING

Reprinted with permission from Ed Preston & Associates

197

Idea Generation: Structured or Unstructured?

❑ **Structured** — Pre-prepared header cards — session leaders have prepared the primary questions and header cards prior to the session. They use those header cards to direct the storyboarding process.

❑ **Unstructured** — No header cards — participants generate ideas on the larger topic and when the idea generation process is finished, they look for clusters of ideas and begin to organize the ideas and develop the header cards from the process.

❑ **Read the headers and ask for ideas:** The facilitator keeps the ideas flowing by asking the header questions, repeating ideas as they are generated, limiting the length of discussion, directing killer balls at negative or killer phrases, and stimulating additional ideas with leading phrases such as: *What about that? . . . Are there other possibilities? . . . How else could you look at that? . . . Does that make you think of other ideas?*

Moving into Evaluation:

❑ **Take a break** — Separate the creative, idea generation phase from the evaluation phase.

❑ **Evaluation guidelines** — Raise objections, be judgmental, look for quality, attack ideas not people, eliminate duplicates, make deletions, prioritize and reorganize.

❑ **Consensus dotting** — Give each participant three dots (votes) to spend on the most important idea or ideas under each header. Participants can vote all three dots on one idea if desired.

❑ **Make report** — Collect the cards in order of importance and prepare a report that shows the headers and ideas generated for each topic.

Materials:

- ❐ Storyboards — 1" styrofoam building insulation boards 4' x 8' cut in half. Cover with cloth. Four or five boards per session.
- ❐ Push pins — 5/8" if possible, 100 for each board.
- ❐ Topic Cards — 5" x 7" blue index cards
- ❐ Header Cards — 4" x 6" salmon index cards
- ❐ Idea Cards — 4" x 6" yellow index cards
- ❐ Felt tip markers — wide point one color for ideas, one color for consensus dotting.

Project Documentation

Storyboards have become a standard part of the total quality process as a way to map out an improvement process and document the progress of that project. In this application, they are used more as a roadmap and communication tool than an idea generation tool.

At West Paces Ferry Hospital storyboards are an integral part of their team improvement projects, called FOCUS-PDCA. The first letter of the process, "F" stands for Find a process to improve. They don't wait for a problem to surface, they go looking for things that could be better. And, there's always something that can be better. Storyboards are everywhere in the hospital and once a month they are displayed in the cafeteria and celebrated by the entire organization. They have used the process in all areas of the hospital, from reducing the number of caesarian deliveries to improving the quality and delivery of sandwiches in the cafeteria.

The storyboard as it is used in the quality improvement process has a specific format which forms a pattern of communication. Because all storyboards show the various pieces of information in a consistent format, people from other parts of the organization, or other organizations entirely, can "read" the storyboard and understand the project and the status of the project. The following is the typical format with an overview of the questions that would be answered by information in each section. Following the illustration is a more complete list of the questions to be answered by each segment of the storyboard.

Typical Storyboard Format

FIND a process: - Who is Customer? - Describe process? - Key issues? - Major process issues? - Who would benefit? - Total system fit? - Who should be involved?	**CLARIFY** current knowledge - What are process boundaries? - Actual flow of process? - Expected outcomes? - Obvious inefficiencies?

ORGANIZE a team
- How many?
- What skills needed?
- Involve customers?
- Who cares?
- Who knows?

UNDERSTAND variation causes
- Major causes?
- Measurement of key variables?
- Improve which causes?

SELECT the project
- Biggest return potential?
- Most feasible?

ROADMAP
- Key Actions?
- Timetable?
- Limitations?
- Progress indicators?
- Available resources?

PLAN the project
- Who, what, when, where, how?
- Pilot project?
- Training?
- Data collection?

DO the improvement
- Collect data
- Analyze results

ACT
- Standardize changes?
- Revise policies?
- Communicate?
- What's next?

CHECK results
- New information?
- Resistance where?
- Variance from plan?
- Expectations met?
- Possible improvements?

Typical Storyboard Format

F: FIND a process to improve —
Why does this process represent an opportunity for improvement?
Is there a clear, simple description of the process improvement opportunity?
What are the major process problems?
What are the key issues?
How does the improvement of this process meet our strategic objectives?
Who will benefit from the improvement?
What other groups are involved with the process?

O: ORGANIZE a team that knows the process —
Who understands the process and cares about it?
Who has expert knowledge of the process?
Who works closest to the process?
Should customers (internal or external) be involved?
How big should the team be?

C: CLARIFY current knowledge of the process —
What are the boundaries of the process?
What is the actual flow of the process?
What are the expected outcomes of the process?
Are there obvious redundancies or inefficiencies?

U: UNDERSTAND the causes of process variation/poor quality —
What are the major causes leading to inefficiency?
What key characteristics of the process are measurable?
Which causes can be improved?

S: SELECT the process improvement —
What improvement opportunity represents the biggest return?
Which improvement opportunity is the most feasible?
What is the Mission Statement for the project?

Team Roadmap
What are the key actions?
What is the approximate timetable?
How will the team determine progress?
What are limitations or obstacles?
What other resources are available?
What measurements will be displayed?

P: PLAN the process improvement
Who, what, when, where, how will the improvement
be made?
Is there a pilot program for the change?
What training will be needed?
Is more data collection necessary?

D: DO the improvement, data collection and analysis

C: CHECK the results and lessons learned
What new data or information was uncovered in the
"doing?"
Where did the plan meet resistance?
How did the implementation vary from the plan?
Did the process improve as expected?
How could the process be improved?
What lessons were learned?
What changes need to be made?

**A: ACT to maintain the improvement or make
needed changes**
What parts of the improvement process can be adopted
and standardized?
What policies or procedures need to be revised?
Who needs to be trained?
Who needs to know about the change?
What measurements need to be continued in order to
maintain the improvement?
What's the next step?

Limitations of Storyboarding

While storyboarding can be extremely effective for idea
generation, it can be a relatively linear, verbal process which
doesn't push participants into new areas of creativity. It is
important to stimulate divergent thinking in order to get the full
benefit of this tool.

One of the first requirements of a divergent thinking
session is to get participants into a different mindspace . . . away
from thoughts of phones, deadlines, and office politics. Some
facilitators lead a short guided imagery to loosen the linear grip on
the minds of participants. This could be a "perfect world" imagery

where people imagine the most perfect product, service, or solution to the problem. Or the imagery could focus on relaxation, visualization, freedom, or color. Many facilitators hesitate to use guided imagery because they fear the attendees will not participate or will consider it too "touchy-feely." However, groups generally enjoy these short (5-minutes or less) mind excursions. Each group is different so facilitators should evaluate the situation and group.

If you decide to try imagery, here are four which have been found to be popular and effective. There are many variations on these available in books on imagery or in many training books. You can also quickly write your own guided imagery to meet your particular needs.

"Breathing" — from *Put Your Mother on the Ceiling* by Richard de Mille —participants breathe in rose petals and raindrops and little lions . . . it's a unique experience. Exercises visualization skills.

"Color Escalator" — participants descend through a rainbow of colors on an escalator, being surrounded by each color at the various levels. Color helps stimulate idea generation.

"Butterfly" — participants experience the feelings of metamorphosis from a caterpillar to a butterfly. Good for situations involving change.

"Favorite Place" — participants visualize their favorite place and spend a few minutes experiencing it with each of their senses. Excellent relaxation exercise. Michael Munn, Ph.D., Director of Creativity for Lockheed Missiles & Space Company, Inc., states, "I got into this business because I started working with Total Quality Management and quickly discovered that TQM didn't do much if people didn't think differently than they thought before. I started trying to find whatever tools I could to help people think differently. In order to get people to see things differently, I have them stare at mandalas or have the group think about *Total Planetary Quality* to expand their thinking or find deep metaphors to compare their company, future or problem to. What I'm trying to accomplish is light-speed paradigm shifts."

There are many techniques which can be used to stimulate divergent thinking. Here are just a few:

❐ Have a short mindmapping session prior to the storyboarding. To force more visual thinking, insist that the participants use only symbols or images for their mindmapping. Have the participants discuss their mindmaps in small groups once they're finished.

❐ Have the group mindmap a "perfect world" for the situation you will be storyboarding.

❐ At some point during the idea generation stage of storyboarding, have the group think of five "stupid and ridiculous" ideas.

❐ Use any of the divergent thinking ideas from Chapter 4 that make sense for your situation.

When combined with divergent thinking stimulators, storyboarding is a powerful thinking tool which incorporates the four fundamentals of group thinking (Participative-Visual-Moveable-Fun) and can be used in all transformation thinking tasks. It stimulates idea generation as well as facilitating idea evaluation and selection. This technique should become a standard thinking tool in all organizations.

Chapter Mindmap

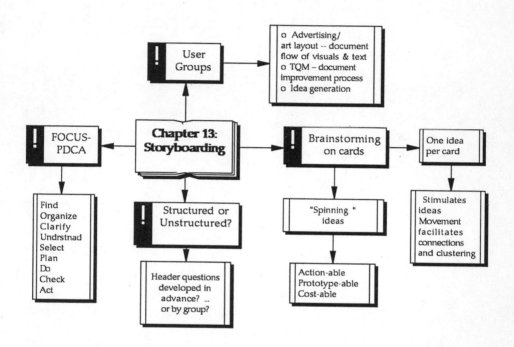

User Groups

o Advertising/
art layout -- document
flow of visuals & text
o TQM – document
improvement process
o Idea generation

FOCUS-PDCA

**Chapter 13:
Storyboarding**

Brainstorming
on cards

One idea
per card

Find
Organize
Clarify
Undrstnad
Select
Plan
Do
Check
Act

Structured or
Unstructured?

"Spinning "
ideas

Stimulates
ideas
Movement
facilitates
connections
and clustering

Header questions
developed in
advance? ...
or by group?

Action-able
Prototype-able
Cost-able

STORYBOARDING

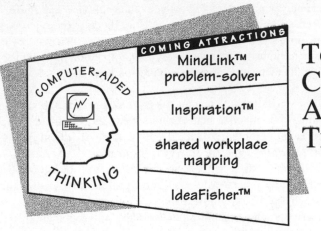

CHAPTER 14

TOOL:
COMPUTER-
AIDED
THINKING

Tasks: Making things better
Making leaps
Concordant decision making
Project management
Training
Communication

You are today where your thoughts have brought you;
you will be tomorrow where your thoughts take you.
— James Allen

Computers have had an enormous impact on our thinking abilities. As personal computers with spreadsheet and data base software became accessible to almost everyone, we started to think more logically and analytically. Spreadsheet software's structure forced our thinking into certain patterns, using rows and columns to analyze data. As computer speed and storage capacity increased, we gained the ability to play "what if" on any quantifiable question. We started gathering more data, cutting information in different ways to discover its lessons, and became far more sophisticated at analyzing and evaluating. We also discovered the fallacy of spreadsheets . . . regardless of how professional the output looks, it's only as good as its input.

Database management software helped us gather even more information and think in terms of records and data fields, searching and sorting. In terms of our "two thinkers" these software products are for "Jud" . . . the judge who likes to gather and analyze data, think logically, evaluate choices and make selections based on linear criteria. Until recently there has been very little software available for "Gen" . . . the idea generator who wants to brainstorm, make leaps, play with color and pictures and leave the evaluation and selection to someone else.

Recently the market has produced several "thoughtware products" designed to help generate ideas and stimulate a creative approach to problem solving. Three products stand out from the rest: *MindLink Problem Solver*™, *Inspiration*™ and *IdeaFisher*™. *MindLink*™, based on the Synectics theories of idea generation, helps people generate ideas and solve problems by leading them through a series of mind-expanding exercises. *Inspiration*™ is a versatile product that allows individuals and groups to do electronic mindmapping for a wide variety of thinking tasks. *IdeaFisher*™ is a thesaurus-like product that is extremely useful for idea generation and strategic thinking.

MindLink Problem Solver™

You know something's different as soon as you open the *MindLink*™ box. Included with the standard disks and documentation is a small black velvet bag that contains several small toys (you could call them idea joggers, which is what they are, but your co-workers will undoubtedly call them toys).

The *MindLink*™ manual is also somewhat more in touch with the average software user than other manuals. After a brief welcome, the manual begins, "If you don't read manuals..." And, you really don't have to read the manual to use this program. But, if you do read the manual, you'll find a concise description of the thinking theories used by the software, as well as a well-written description of how to use it productively.

MindLink™ is designed to get your creative juices flowing. It is divided into four parts: the Gym, Idea Generation, Guided Problem Solving and Problem Solving. The Gym is a place to go to limber up your mind. A typical exercise has you think of possible uses for a common object (such as a nickel or a coffee cup). Then you think of applications that the object couldn't possibly fit. After going through those processes, the program forces a thinking stretch by having you think of ways to make the object fit those impossible uses.

Because you're totally alone with your computer (which never laughs at you or tells you your ideas are stupid) there is a great freedom to put down any ideas regardless of logic or quality. In one exercise we went through, we were thinking of uses and impossible applications for a coffee cup. One of our impossible uses was as an airplane. *MindLink*™ stretched us to make a connection between a coffee cup and an airplane. Our mental fantasy tied a line from the coffee cup to a hot air balloon then placed a mouse in the cup. The mouse thought he was in an airplane! Maybe not a brilliant thought but it definitely loosened our thinking processes.

The Gym helps take away inhibitions and allows new possibilities. The kicker comes at the end of the exercise when the system presents you with a score! There is an immediate flash of "I could have thought of more ideas." Which, of course, is the point . . . we can always think of more ideas.

The Idea Generation and Problem Solving sections of *MindLink*™ allow you to apply idea generation techniques to your specific problems. One example comes from John Nevison, a principal with Duncan-Nevison a consulting firm which specializes in project management. Nevison used *MindLink*™ to help him develop a two-day course on project management. He explains, "A phenomenon that has always interested me about projects is that the time period just before the deadline is when you could use more people to help get the job done. But the practicality is that you can't hire people then. It would take too long to bring them up to speed. So the only alternative is to put the pedal to the metal and finish the project."

With that scenario in mind, Nevison worked through *MindLink's* Guided Problem Solving which presented him with a poem about getting through the mountains. This poem triggered a thought process for Nevison. "The last stage of a project is like the last leg of a wagon train journey that must go through Death Valley," Nevison stated. "You've got to get all your materials together before you make the final push across the desert."

Nevison used the wagon train metaphor throughout his course and has also used it in talks and articles as a way to make his theories and ideas more understandable.

One of *MindLink's* first exercises in the problem solving

session is to have the user develop a wish list. By concentrating on an ideal outcome, the mind is concentrated on possibilities rather than barriers or limitations. *MindLink* is an excellent thinking tool for triggering new ideas and different trains of thought. It is also fun and simple to use.

Inspiration™

Craig Ellerbroek, Director of Advanced Programming with Martin Marietta Information Systems, manages a research and development budget that is never big enough to meet all the potential needs. His challenge is to maximize "customer" (internal and external) satisfaction with limited, frequently changing resources. In a recent interview, Ellerbroek stated, "We needed to do a consolidated research and development plan knowing we had multiple customers, diverse views and a wish list that was far bigger than our coffers. The process we used was what I call real-time brainstorming. We brought together a group of about fifteen people whose buy-in we needed. We met for several 2-3 hour sessions at one of our laboratories. Each lab has an electronic meeting environment equipped with *Inspiration*™ and a person trained to use the software and gather input quickly and accurately. We also used a professional facilitator to keep the process moving.

"The primary advantage of the process was the consensus we achieved. Sitting in a room together and being able to instantly see all the ideas and concerns of everyone else made the negotiation a process of idea generation and problem solving rather than a turf battle. In a relatively short time we reached a consensus that was so strong that the participants felt comfortable going back and pitching the plan to their organizations. Consensus was the main thing I was after because the processes we had used before this time had never really achieved true agreement. We would draft a plan, send it out to the parties for input, try to incorporate the suggestions and send it out again. It never made everyone happy and the agreements would fall apart over minor issues because, basically, they never had a real agreement or consensus.

"For me, the proof of the process came when we had changes. R&D budgets often change and in a normal cycle, the change prompts a complete renegotiation — either of how to spend the increase or what to cut if it's a decrease. Every adjustment would always take us back to the drawing board with everybody fighting for their personal interests. When we had a change after going through the real-time brainstorming session, I called everyone back together and two hours later they came out with an answer. I told them they were almost making the process too easy."

Ellerbroek concludes, "I believe technology such as *Inspiration*™ is an enabler not an answer. One of the advantages it offers is that it puts thoughts and ideas into an electronic form which means that not everyone has to be in the original meeting to gain concensus. You can distribute the mindmap created by *Inspiration* to a wider audience and ask for additional input. They can easily add a bubble or color-code a section so it makes it easier to think together across the organization."

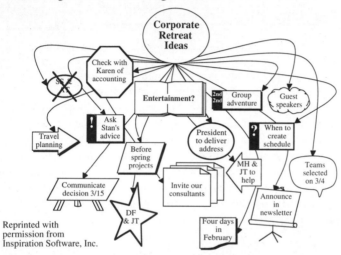

Reprinted with permission from Inspiration Software, Inc.

For years people asked us if mindmapping could be computerized and we said we didn't think so. The very nature of mindmapping is a fast, visual "dumping" of information. Putting a machine between mind and paper seemed to be an obstruction. Obviously, someone at *Inspiration* had a much more open mind (namely, founder Mona Westhaver!).

MacWorld (February, 1993) rates *Inspiration* with four stars and *MacUser* (June, 1993) stated: *Our brainstorming tool of choice is Inspiration*™*, a whizbang outliner and free-form-diagram generator ... like getting two programs in one.* Originally developed as a visual thinking tool for the Apple Macintosh, *Inspiration* is now also available for use in a Microsoft® Windows™ environment.

211

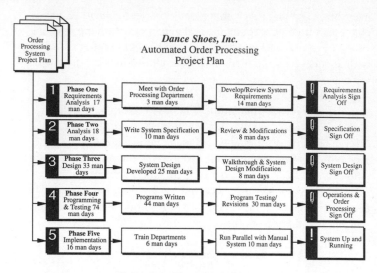

Reprinted with permission from Inspiration Software, Inc.

Inspiration is an idea development tool used for individual and group brainstorming, creating diagrams and writing. It integrates easy-to-use diagramming and powerful outlining software and makes it easy to switch back and forth between the two views. It facilitates visual thinking with colors, symbols and easy moveability of the information. *Inspiration* can be used to create idea maps, flow charts, tree charts, presentation visuals, outlines, proposals, stories and reports. It reveals themes, patterns and relationships to the information and simplifies the communication of complex information.

This powerful software is designed for visual thinking right on the computer. Its free-form visual environment helps stimulate thinking while revealing relationships, thought patterns, themes, ideas and new perspectives. The software facilitates a rapid brainstorming process (called Rapid-Fire) which can be used individually or, when projected on a screen, it can be used in groups to record ideas far faster and more effectively than the standard recorder with a pen. In the brainstorming mode, *Inspiration* allows the thinker(s) to enter information and have idea balloons pop-up on the screen as fast as the information is entered.

Diagrams of all kinds are easy to create and modify with this software — presentation visuals, flow charts, organization charts and Total Quality Management diagrams. These diagrams help explain and communicate ideas, procedures, projects and structures. "Sticky Links" keep symbols connected when they are moved. Pre-defined symbols make it easy to differentiate processes, levels, responsibilities or operations.

Inspiration's visual maps instantly turn into organized outlines which simplify any type of writing project . . . business reports, proposals, sales letters, brochures . . . even novels and plays. The outliner function lets you quickly add, rearrange and organize your writing.

Inspiration should become a standard piece of software on every computer, joining the big three (wordprocessing, spreadsheet, and data base management) as the minimum software requirement.

IdeaFisher™

**Tomorrow's world is determined by the ideas created today.
— Marsh Fisher, founder, IdeaFisher Systems, Inc.**

Marsh Fisher has been a serious student of creativity since 1964 when he attended a humor writing class at UCLA. Fisher discovered that he lacked the ability to ad-lib and generate ideas as quickly as his fellow students. Often as he drove home, a funny idea would come to mind and he would wonder why he couldn't think of those ideas in class.

His search for "why" led him to the seeds of *IdeaFisher™*. One of the comedy writing techniques taught in the class involved generating a list of ideas associated with a given comedy situation. When several writers participated, the list was full of variety and contained more ideas than any single individual would have thought of alone. As Fisher pursued the elusive ability to make creative connections, he realized that his own production of creative ideas was limited primarily by his memory abilities and the variety of associations which were generated by his life experience.

Fisher's study confirmed that these limitations were not just his. In general, the human mind has a much higher ability to recognize information than to recall it. This is one reason multiple choice tests are so much easier than essay exams. Fisher believed that the limitations to recall and the lack of association variety were ones that could be overcome with the help of computer software. Therefore, when he retired as co-founder of Century 21 Real Estate Corporation in 1977, he began to work full-time on the idea of a software package that would help people generate ideas by expanding their limited memory capabilities, helping them make associations and asking probing questions.

Through his years of studying the creative process, Fisher concluded:

> *Creativity is about as magical as the skill required to add two plus two. Both can be taught and learned. And the more one practices any discipline, the more proficient one becomes.*

The software package that resulted from his research is a 25 megabyte associative database (compressed to 7 megabytes) designed to stimulate thinking about anything and capable of being tailored by the user to include industry- or product-specific terms and links. The award-winning software contains two databases uniquely arranged and linked:

❐ **QBank** — contains nearly 6,000 questions organized to clarify problems, modify ideas, and evaluate solutions.

❐ **IdeaBank** — contains over 70,000 idea words with nearly 800,000 associated links. It is somewhat like a huge free-associated thesaurus.

The psychological foundation of *IdeaFisher* rests on the principles of association, memory retrieval, and the use of analogy and metaphor. Thinkers interact with and use the idea words to stimulate ideas and associations in their own memory banks. New connections and associations are stimulated and a tremendous number of ideas can be generated in an extremely short period of time.

According to Fisher, the creative thinking process consists of three major steps which he calls "The New Three Rs." Each step depends on the success of the previous one. Together they act synergistically to produce new ideas. The steps are:

1. **Recording information** (committing it to memory). Highly creative people are also highly curious and

generally knowledgeable about many subjects. They
mentally file vast amounts of information.

2. **Retrieving information** (recalling, reconstructing it). This
is the most difficult, unreliable step. It is entirely
dependent upon what has been recorded but regardless of
how much has been recorded, the retrieval process is often
haphazard and error-prone. You may know the name of
your next door neighbor almost as well as your own yet, in
a moment of stress, be completely unable to remember it.
Almost everyone has had the frustration of having a name
or piece of information "on the tip of their tongue" yet not
being able to retrieve it.

3. **Recombining information** (putting it together in a
different way). New ideas are almost always the result of
recombining existing ideas or parts of ideas in a new way.
Marcel Proust, the French philosopher said: *The real
voyage of discovery consists not in seeking new lands but
in having new eyes.* Before information can be
recombined, it must have been recorded and be
retrievable.

IdeaFisher speeds up the creative process, mimicking the
way the human mind organizes and remembers experiences by
using associations to link words and concepts together. These idea
associations provoke different mental images about the subject
being considered, and stimulate new viewpoints and ideas. These
associations can be used to generate ideas for new products or
services, new markets or uses for existing products or services,
advertising or promotional campaigns, special events or programs,
training programs, presentations, stories or scripts, and corporate or
product names.

One of the examples of how *IdeaFisher* works is given in
the Introduction to the software manual. If you were stuck trying to
think of something to fix for dinner, you could sit with a blank
piece of paper in front of you and hope for an idea . . . or you could
go to the grocery story and wander through the thousands of items
displayed and generate hundreds of ideas that could be mixed,
matched, accepted or discarded. Using *IdeaFisher*™ is like walking
through a supermarket. You can scroll through the IdeaBank and
collect ideas and associations that come to you as you browse
through the thousands of idea words related to the concept you're
thinking about.

A more real-world example of the use of *IdeaFisher* comes from Jim Shenk, manager of contracts and program management with CEC Instruments in San Dimas, CA, who used the software to facilitate a strategic planning process. "We needed to do some strategic thinking for the division so we used *IdeaFisher* to help guide us through the process. The first thing it does is ask the questions that are so obvious that you usually don't ask them . . . and, all too often, don't really know the answer to . . . such as *What business are we in?* and *Why do our customers buy from us? IdeaFisher* offers nearly 6,000 questions to help stimulate thinking.

"We asked ourselves a lot of questions and the answers began to lead us toward an opportunity. We have been heavily dependent on the aerospace industry and this opportunity helped us create a market outside that industry, in the commercial aviation market.

"I've also used the software to help set up a mission statement and for understanding what our business is all about. It was extremely helpful for thinking through those questions. I also use the Strategic Planning Module, which has a lot of interesting questions specifically organized for planning, as well as the Presentation Planning Module. (There is also a Business and Grant Proposal Module available.)

"It's important to remember that *IdeaFisher* doesn't create anything for you. It's not like a spread sheet or a database program that will produce something. *IdeaFisher* just helps stimulate your own thinking and keeps you focused on questions that most of us tend to think are too obvious to even be considered. In actual fact, we can't answer many of those questions because we really haven't thought about them . . . and when we do think about them enough to answer them, we find they lead us in directions that we might not have discovered before.

"When we use *IdeaFisher*, we look for related topics and let the various idea words stimulate thoughts and associations. We're in a high-tech niche so we've added a lot of stuff to the database to make it even more useful to us. It also provides an electronic scratchpad which allows you to capture the ideas as you work through the process.

"When times are tough, I think it's even more important

to use this type of thinking tool to make sure you're not overlooking a potential problem or a new opportunity. Sometimes in tough times it seems like we get stuck even more in our old patterns of thinking — *This worked before so it should work again.* That way of thinking has always sort of baffled me because obviously what we did before isn't working now or we wouldn't be in this mess ... so what we need to do is something different from what we were doing. *IdeaFisher* is a great way to find 100 new ideas ... even if you reject 99 of them, so what? If you get one that's useable or opens up a new opportunity, it makes the process worthwhile."

Clayton Lee, Houston-based inventor of the Orbiter, an impact-free trampoline treadmill, used *IdeaFisher* to reduce the unit-cost of an add-on to the Orbiter . . . from $2,000 a unit to approximately $100 per unit. The vast reduction in cost opened up new markets and Lee stated, "*IdeaFisher* puts more thinking back into the marketplace. It helps develop our minds, which is something we've forgotten how to do. Thinking is no longer an elective skill."

Ron Sargent, a fluid engineer who designed the first cruise control for GM, the Port-A-Potty and the Dancing Waters at Disney World's EPCOT Center, states, "We look at *IdeaFisher* almost as an open-ended platform, an AutoCAD for creativity."

IdeaFisher is a powerful thinking tool which has been used in a wide variety of ways. In addition to the examples given above, *IdeaFisher* has been used to write sermons, design tapestries, develop university courses, create product names, and to invent a tree shaker modification for the orchard industry. It has even played a part in Vice President Al Gore's reinventing government project where it was used by the Department of Commerce in a series of focus group meetings to help transform complaints into suggestions.

The Idea Center®

Bob Martin, co-founder of International Business Resources, Inc., decided to put the powerful combination of *Inspiration*™ and *IdeaFisher*™ together with an ideal thinking environment to create an "Idea Center™" — a place that would facilitate the generation of ideas, strategic planning, problem solving, process improvement and communication. The Idea Center® consists of a meeting room with a semi-circular table, six Macintosh computers interlinked to each other and to a projection system, a meeting facilitator, and an "electographer," a person who helps capture all the information in the computer system and several pieces of thoughtware linked together with a "meeting navigator" — a piece of software developed by IBR.

"We wanted to create a new ecology for the way meetings happen," states Martin. "We designed a physical environment where all the theories of creativity and problem solving can happen easily and naturally . . . a place where magic happens. Some of our clients report productivity increases of up to 400%." Richard Mowrey of Management Services & Development Limited was astonished at the efficiency of an Idea Center session. He stated, "It was simply amazing that we could accomplish so much in such a short period."

"One of the things we find especially effective is the visual mapping of the information," Martin explains. "It keeps all of the pieces of information in front of the participants where it can trigger other thoughts even much later in the thinking process. The information is always in an available and accessible format. Ideas and information don't get lost."

One recent Idea Center client was a molding company that wanted to chart a course for a newly acquired company which had been defunct for about a year when the client company acquired it. Six board members, the CEO of another subsidiary company and the new CEO of the acquisition company met for two days to look at markets and marketing strategy.

Most of the first day was spent in "shared workspace mapping" (with *Inspiration*) looking at their world in the year 2000. They looked at the company, the environment, customers, government, threats, technology and other issues that would impact the company in the future. Once they decided what the company would look like in year 2000, they could work backward from that future view and build a plan to get there.

Martin states, "The group was very satisfied with this Back-to-the-Future process because it unearthed some ideas they felt would not have been considered. They spent about four hours generating marketing ideas on day two and used a random phrase

from *IdeaFisher* to trigger ideas. The phrase was Book of the
Month Club and we filled a screen with qualities of that phrase . . .
trial offers, negative acceptance, catalog, etc. Out of this exercise
came a breakthrough marketing concept that had never before been
used in their industry (and, therefore, can't be discussed until it is
released)."

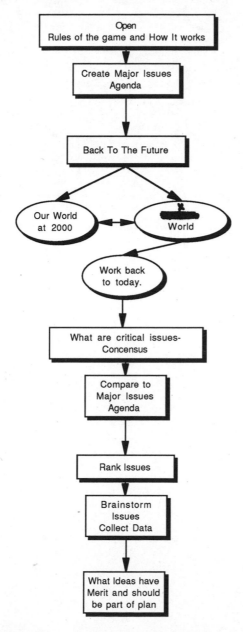

Reprinted with permission from IBR

Shared Workspace Mapping

"Shared workspace mapping" is Martin's term for the projection of the idea generation process through a computer interface onto a screen. A primary benefit of this mapping process is that everyone in the room sees the ideas as they are presented. They see their own ideas mingling with the ideas of everyone else. Gradually the ownership of the ideas is less important than the shaping, developing, extending and expanding of the ideas themselves.

This process is available to any organization even without the high-tech facility developed by Martin. The minimum requirement for the process is as follows:

❑ Personal computer, Macintosh or IBM

❑ *Inspiration* (Add *IdeaFisher* for more idea generation power)

❑ LCD Overhead Projection Panel and software

❑ Electographer (someone fluent in the software programs and use of the hardware who can capture ideas quickly and accurately

❑ Laser printer or access to one so that hard copies can be generated frequently.

At the beginning of the session, brief the attendees about the process and run them through a short demonstration of how the system works. You may want to prepare questionnaires prior to the session to start people thinking about the questions that will be discussed. Also have a template of where you're going so the attendees can stay focused on the process. Martin's group has developed over 200 templates to facilitate the thinking process in almost any situation.

Reminder

It's important to remember one caveat to using these important software products. It's what *MacWorld* states at the beginning of its review of *Inspiration*: *Brainstorming (thinking) capabilities are only as good as the users.* Scott DeGarmo, editor of *Success* magazine which uses *IdeaFisher* in its brainstorming sessions, echoes this belief and emphasizing the fact that Computer-Aided Thinking programs are not a push-the-button-and-out-pops the answer type of solution. He states: *It's (IdeaFisher™) based on the theory that the more ideas you produce, the more likely it is you'll have a good idea. It's a catalyst.*

Alan Kay, one of the Macintosh visionaries, believes that one of the ways computers will help us in the future is by suggesting alternatives. *Regardless of what you asked for, it would come up with another way, just to remind you there is more than one way of looking at something.* The computer doesn't think for us but using these software packages can help us think more effectively . . . which isn't a bad return for a relatively small investment.

Chapter Mindmap

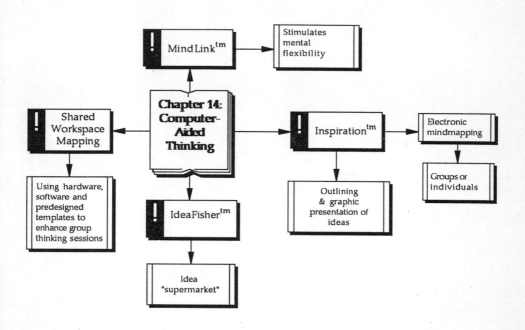

THE
TRANSFORMATION
JOURNEY

Diamonds in Our Back Yard

In South Africa a young man longed to make his fortune so he left his farm and headed for the diamond fields. For years he prospected to no avail, finally returning home weary and penniless. And, as the well-known story goes, one day the broken, depressed man happened to be digging in his back yard when he discovered an enormously rich deposit of . . . diamonds, of course.

Apocryphal or not, this story fits human nature. (The originator of the story was Civil War veteran Russell Conwell who raised several million dollars using it in his speeches and eventually founded Temple University in Philadelphia with his fortune.) We have a tendency to look for riches in "other places." The grass is always greener somewhere else: an untested product has unlimited possibilities, the not-yet-hired employee/associate is always more productive and less worrisome than the ones we've worked with for years, and the next new system is bound to be better than the one we tried yesterday. It's time to quit gazing over the fence and look for the diamonds in our own backyard.

We haven't yet learned how to use our full human potential nor how to work together most effectively. Most scientists believe that we use less than 10% of our mental capability. And most organizational studies reveal that people perform far below their possible standards . . . the standards which utilize 10% or less of their abilities!

Every person within an organization represents a hidden reservoir of potential. We never know where ideas will come from. Jack Stack at Springfield ReManufacturing Company got some of his breakthrough ideas from the janitor! Expecting ideas only from engineering or marketing or the research and development folks is like looking for diamonds only where they've already been found.

We not only have to start looking at every member of our organizations as a source of wealth, but we also need to learn to use more of each person's potential. Organizations have become our most important social environment. We spend more time there than we do at school, at home, or in our churches. Organizations offer us a primary environment for growth, learning and mastery.

In our fast-changing global world, our organizations need to rethink themselves constantly and continuously meet the challenges of changes in markets, technologies, consumer tastes, material availabilities, and information channels. We need an on-going process of transformation which can only come as we become "transformation thinking organizations." Transformation thinking organizations know how to bring every member of the organization into the process of thinking together, learning and growing.

They know that people need to learn and grow and the environment which supports that growth requires the following:

❐ an information-rich and an interaction-rich culture;

❐ a "people first" attitude: respect, trust (truth/ethics), commitment (vision and ownership), and recognition;

❐ highly co-active communication systems that are open, inclusive and multi-sensory.

Transformation organizations know that for transformation to happen, their associates need to know how to think together . . . how to separate idea generation ("Gen") from idea evaluation and selection ("Jud") and how to use the four fundamentals of transformation thinking: participation, visual information, moveable information, fun. And, they help all of their associates learn how to use the transformation thinking tools: brainstorming, brainwriting, fishboning, mess mapping, mindmapping and mindscaping, sticky charting, storyboarding and the computer-aided thinking tools that fit the task.

It all boils down to this simple formula: put people first, give them the tools they need and teach them how to use them. Graphically, it looks like this:

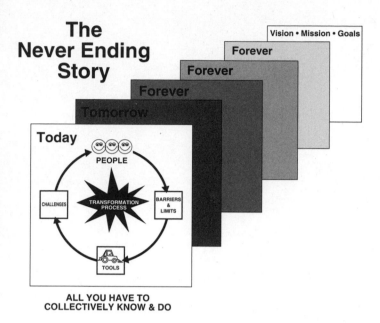

Transformation thinking organizations know that learning to think together better is an on-going process not a quick fix. It's a journey not a destination. We would like to encourage you to embark on this journey and find the diamonds buried in your backyard.

TRANSFORMATION READING LIST

Leadership and the New Science, Learning About Organization from an Orderly Universe, by Margaret J. Wheatley, Berrett-Koehler, 1992.
A small book with a major impact. Takes a little time to assimilate all the thoughts in this book but it's worth it.

Lateral Thinking, Creativity Step by Step, by Edward de Bono, Harper & Row, 1970.
The godfather of creativity . . . not the most fun reading in the world but loaded with good stuff.

101 Creative Problem Solving Techniques, The Handbook of New Ideas for Business, by James M. Higgins, New Management Publishing Company, Inc., Winter Park, FL, 1994.
An excellent book to keep near whenever you need to stir up your thinking.

Thinkertoys, A Handbook of Business Creativity for the 90s, by Michael Michalko, Ten Speed Press, Berkeley, California, 1991.
Highly readable . . . guaranteed to stimulate some new ideas.

Jump Start Your Brain, by Doug Hall with David Wecker, Warner Books, New York, 1995.
An outrageous book by an outrageous guy . . . a real treat.

What a Great Idea! Key Steps Creative People Take, by Charles "Chic" Thompson, HarperCollins, New York, 1992.
More great ideas about how to improve your organization.

Discovering Common Ground, How Future Search Conferences Bring People Together to Achieve Breakthrough Innovation, Empowerment, Shared Vision and Collaborative Action, by Marvin R. Weisbord, Berrett-Koehler, 1992.
Bring strategic planning sessions alive with the "Future Search" format . . . from a pragmatic thinker who was practicing participative management, cross-functional teams and many other "buzz words" long before they became the "in" thing.

Innovate or Evaporate, Test & Improve Your Organization's IQ: Its Innovation Quotient, by James M. Higgins, New Management Publishing Company, Winter Park, FL, 1995.
An excellent guide to organizational innovation.

Reengineering the Corporation, A Manifesto for Business Revolution, by Michael Hammer & James Champy, HarperBusiness, New York, 1994.
A book that shows how dramatic transformation processes can be.

The Fifth Discipline, The Art & Practice of the Learning Organization, by Peter Senge, Doubleday, 1990.
Must reading although vague on application.

The Great Game of Business, The Only Sensible Way to Run a Company, by Jack Stack, Doubleday, 1992.
Fun, easy-to-read, by an emerging corporate hero who learned the true meaning of Grow or Die. Don't miss this one!

Mindmapping: Your Personal Guide to Exploring Creativity and Problem-Solving, by Joyce Wycoff, Berkley Publishing, New York, 1992.
Guides readers in using this simple technique with many different thinking tasks.

Flow: The Psychology of Optimal Experience, by Mihaly Scikszentimihalyi, Harper & Row, Publishers, New York, 1990.

Creativity in Business, by Michael Ray and Rochelle Myers, Doubleday & Company, Garden City, NY, 1986.
One of the classics in the industry.

Creative Whack Pack, by Roger von Oech, US Games Systems, Inc., Stamford, CT, 1992.
A card deck that can help you come up with winning ideas.

IdeaPower, Techniques & Resources to Unleash the Creativity in Your Organization, by Arthur VanGundy, Ph.D., AMACOM, New York, 1992.
Dozens of techniques for stimulating new ideas.

Grow or Die, The Unifying Principle of Transformation, by George T. Ainsworth Land, Reissued Edition, John Wiley & Sons, New York, 1986.
High fog-factor . . . but worth it!

Break-Point and Beyond, Mastering the Future Today, by George Land and Beth Jarman, HarperBusiness, New York, 1993.

Creative Growth Games, by Eugene Raudsepp
Several other volumes available but hard to find . . . great training ideas.

Conceptual Blockbusting, A Guide to Better Ideas, 2nd Edition, by James L. Adams, Ph. D., W. W. Norton & Company, New York, 1980.
Another classic.

I Know It When I See It, A Modern Fable About Quality, by John Guaspari, AMACOM, New York, 1985.
A delightful little book with a big message.

RESOURCES

Associations

Innovative Thinking Network
1324 State St., G-153
Santa Barbara, CA 93101
805-964-5363 FAX 805-964-6383
A business-oriented association of people focused on individual
and group thinking skills, innovation and creativity

Renaissance Business Associates
Box 418
Boise, ID 83701
208-343-5163
Professional association focused on ethics and integrity in
organizations

International Creativity Network Center
for Studies in Creativity
Buffalo State College
1300 Elmwood Avenue, Chase Hall 244
Buffalo, NY 1422
716-878-6223
Broad spectrum of creativity interests

American Creativity Association
Box 26068
St. Paul, MN 55126-0068
612-784-8375
Promotion of personal and professional creativity.

The Global Intuition Network
University of Texas, El Paso
P.O. Box 614
El Paso, TX 79968-0614
Developing and using intuition in corporate life

Thinking Skills Trainers & Consultants

Jordan Ayan
Create-It!
416 Apple River
Naperville, IL 60565-6300
708-369-6044
 Innovation, new product development, information superhighway

Doug Hall
Richard Saunders International
3851 Edwards Rd.
Cincinnati, OH 45244
513-271-9911
New product brainstorming and market testing

James M. Higgins
James M. Higgins & Associates
400 No. New York Avenue, Suite 215
Winter Park, FL 32789
407-647-5344 FAX: 407-475-575
Organizational innovation

Robert King, Executive Director
GOAL/QPC
13 Branch Street Methuen, MA 01844
800-643-4316,
Books and materials catalog
508-685-3900 FAX: 508-685-6151
Nonprofit organization helping organizations improve quality,
productivity and competitiveness

George Land
Leadership 2000
3602 East Campbell
Phoenix, AZ 85018
602-468-9944 FAX: 602-998-8515
Backwards from Perfect planning; CoNexus

Nancy Margulies
709 Wenneker
St. Louis, MO 63124
314-991-2008 FAX: 314-991-1122
Corporate mindmapping and mindscaping facilitator

Bob Martin
International Business Resources
3450 Penrose, Suite 250
Boulder, CO 80301
303-447-0846 FAX: 303-447-9701
Creative Strategic Planning, The Idea Center®

Jerry McNellis
The McNellis Group
P.O. Box 582
New Brighton, PA 15066
412-847-2120 FAX: 412-847-9275
Compression planning and storyboard training and materials

Anthony G. Nagle
A.G. Nagle Company
4018 West 65th Street, Suite 111
Edina, MN 55435
612-925-4938 FAX: 612-925-5876
Negotiation and sales training, storyboards

Ed Preston, Ed Preston & Associates
4741 Atlantic Boulevard Suite B-2
Jacksonville, FL 32207
904-396-4139
Planning facilitators, storyboards

Tim Richardson
Total Development Resources, Inc.
363-6 Atlantic Blvd., #201
Atlantic Beach, FL 32233-5283
904-249-0919 FAX: 904-249-1861
800-200-0291
Transformation thinking training and consulting, Train-the-trainer
and facilitation training

Charles "Chic" Thompson
Creative Management Group
226 E. High St.
Charlottesville, VA 22902-5177
804-296-6138 FAX: 804-979-4879

Arthur VanGundy, Ph.D.
VanGundy & Associates
428 Laws Dr.
Norman, OK 73072
405-447-1946 FAX: 405-447-1960
Creativity/innovation training

Joyce Wycoff
MindPlay
1324 State St., G-153
Santa Barbara, CA 93101
805-964-5363 FAX: 805-964-6383
Mindmapping and Transformation Thinking training
and consulting

Miscellaneous

Hilton Smith, Director
Foxfire Teacher Outreach
P.O. Box B
Rabun Gap, GA 30568
404-746-5828 FAX: 404-746-5829
Journals, videotapes

National Institute of Standards and Technology
Rte. 270 and Quince Orchard Rd. Administration Bldg, Rm A537
Gaithersburg, MD 20899
301-975-2036
Information about the Malcolm Baldrige Quality Award

Pat Sullivan
Sullivan & Associates
535 Middlefield Road #1100
Menlo Park, CA 94025
415-322-4569
Intellectual capital asset management

Michael Tattersol, President
US Office Scientific Generics
1601 Trapelo Road
Waltham, MA 02154
617-290-0500
Intellectual capital asset management

National Technological University
700 Centre Avenue
Fort Collins, CO 80526-1842
303-495-6400 FAX: 303-484-0668
On-site technical training and college courses

Books, Videos, Audio-tapes, Software

For an extensive listing of resources available to help stimulate and
train creativity, creative problem-solving and thinking skills see the
extensive resource listing in:

*IdeaPower, Techniques & Resources to Unleash the Creativity in
Your Organization,* by Arthur VanGundy, Amacom, New York,
1992.

MindLink, Inc.
Box 247 Kings Highway
North Pomfret, VT 05053
800-253-1844
MindLink Problem Solver™ software

Inspiration Software, Inc.
2920 S.W. Dolph Court, Suite 3
Portland, OR 97219
503-245-9011   800-877-4792
Inspiration™ software

IdeaFisher Systems, Inc.
2222 Martin, #110
Irvine, CA 92715
714-474-8111 FAX: 714-757-2896
 IdeaFisher™ software

Neil Larson
MaxThink™
2425B Channing Way #552
Berkeley, CA 94704
510-540-5508
Excellent, low-cost outlining, hypertext software.

BIBLIOGRAPHY

Section I
The Transformation Environment

Ehrbar, Al, "'Re-Engineering' Gives Firms New Efficiency, Workers the Pink Slip," *Wall Street Journal*, March 16, 1993.

Land, George T. Ainsworth, *Grow or Die, Reissued Edition*, John Wiley & Sons, New York, 1986.

Ludeman, Ph.D., Kate, *The Worth Ethic, How to Profit from the Changing Values of the New Work Force*, E.P. Dutton, New York, 1989.

On Herman Miller, *Annual Report*, 1992.

Chapter 1
Grow or Die

Ashford, Susan J., "Individual Strategies for Coping with Stress During Organizational Transitions," *The Journal of Applied Behavioral Science*, Vol. 24, Number 1/1988, page 19-36.

Dumaine, Brian, "Business Secrets of Tommy Lasorda," *Fortune*, July 3, 1989.

"How to Focus Your Managers on the Exact Skills That Will Make Continuous Improvement Happen," *Quality Digest*, September, 1991.

Lammers, Teri, "The Effective Employee Feedback System," *INC.*, February, 1993, p. 109-11.

Weisbord, Marvin R., *Productive Workplaces, Organizing and Managing for Dignity, Meaning, and Community*, Jossey-Bass Publishers, San Francisco, 1991.

Chapter 2
People First!

Ackoff, Russell, *Management in Small Doses*, John Wiley & Sons, Inc., New York, 1986.

Ansberry, Clare, "Steelmakers Find a Cost-Cutting Plan Yields Headaches," *Wall Street Journal*, March 17, 1993.

Beales, Janet, "Job and School Under One Roof," *Nation's Business*, February, 1993, p. 55-56.

Guaspari, John, *I Know It When I See It, A Modern Fable About Quality*, Amacom, New York, 1985.

Harrell, Wilson, *For Entrepreneurs Only*, Career Press, 1994.

Honold, Linda, "The Power of Learning at Johnsonville Foods," *Training*, April 1991, p. 55-58.

Klose, Kevin, *Russia and the Russians, Inside the Closed Society*, Norton, New York, 1986.

Lang, Sarah, "Corning's Blueprint for Training in the '90s," *Training*, July, 1991, p. 33-36.

Quinn, James Brian, *Intelligent Enterprise, A Knowledge and Service Based Paradigm for Industry*, The Free Press, New York, 1992.

Schutz, Will, *The Truth Option*, 10 Speed Press, Berkeley, CA, 1984.

Stewart, Thomas A., "Brainpower," *Fortune*, June 3, 1991.

Welles, Edward O., "Captain Marvel," *INC.*, January 1992.

Chapter 3
Communicate . . . Communicate . . . Communicate!

Rhodes, Lucien, with Amend, Patricia, "The Turnaround," *INC.*, August, 1986.

Stack, Jack, Edited by Burlingame, Bo, *The Great Game of Business*, Doubleday Currency, New York, 1992.

Weisbord, Marvin R., *Productive Workplaces, Organizing and Managing for Dignity, Meaning, and Community*, Jossey-Bass Publishers, San Francisco, 1991.

"Why I Hate Being the Boss," Interview with Jack Stack, *INC.*, October 1989.

Section II
Transformation Thinking

Wigginton, Eliot, *Sometimes a Shining Moment, The Foxfire Experience*, Anchor Press/Doubleday, Garden City, NY, 1985.

Chapter 4
Two Thinkers

Boostrom, Robert Ph.D., *Developing Creative & Critical Thinking, An Integrated Approach*, National Textbook Company, Lincolnwood, IL, 1992.

De Bono, Edward, Sur/Petition, *Creating Value Monopolies When Everyone Else Is Merely Competing*, HarperBusiness, New York, 1992.

Steel, Dawn, *They Can Kill You ... But They Can't Eat You, Lessons from the Front*, Pocket Books, New York, 1993.

Thompson, Charles "Chic," *What a Great Idea! Key Steps Creative People Take*, HarperPerennial, New York, 1992.

Von Oech, Ph.D., Roger, *A Whack on the Side of the Head, How to Unlock Your Mind for Innovation*, Warner Books, New York, 1983.

Wujec, Tom, *Pumping Ions, Games and Exercises to Flex Your Mind*, Doubleday and Company, Inc., Garden City, NY, 1988.

Wycoff, Joyce, *Mindmapping: Your Personal Guide to Exploring Creativity and Problem-Solving*, Berkley Publishing Group, New York, 1991.

Chapter 5
Thinking Together

Kanon, Sharon, "Visual Smarts," *World Press Review*, January, 1992.

Michalko, Michael, *Thinkertoys, A Handbook of Business Creativity for the '90s*, Ten Speed Press, Berkeley, CA, 1991.

"Motorola: Big Doesn't Necessarily Mean Slow," *Wall Street Journal*, December 9, 1992.

Senge, Peter, *The Fifth Discipline, The Art and Practice of the Learning Organization*, Doubleday Currency, New York, 1990.

"You Think Faster on Your Feet," *MindPlay*, Volume 3, Issue 8, October, 1989.

Chapter 6
Eight Thinking Pitfalls to Avoid

Cathcart, Jim, *The Acorn Principle*, unpublished manuscript.

Dawson, Roger, *Confident Decision Making*, Nightengale-Conant, (audio series).

Dumaine, Brian, "What the Leaders of Tomorrow See," *Fortune*, July 3, 1989.

Nightengale, Bob, "Bargain Basement," *Los Angeles Times*, April 3, 1993.

The Role of Intuition in Decision Making (video), *The Global Intuition Network*, 1992

Sellers, Patricia, "The Dumbest Marketing Ploy," *Fortune*, October 5, 1992.

Section III
Power Thinking Tools

Chapter 7
Tool: Better Brainstorming

A Collection of 84 Ideas for Teachers by Teachers, 3M Commercial Office Supply Division, 1993.

VanGundy, Ph.D., Arthur, "Overcoming Productivity Losses in Brainstorming and Brainwriting Groups," research paper in progress, 1993.

Chapter 8
Tool: Brainwriting

VanGundy, Ph.D., Arthur, *Idea Power, Techniques & Resources to Unleash the Creativity in Your Organization*, Amacom, New York, 1992.

Chapter 9
Tool: Mess Mapping

Ackoff, Russell, *Management in Small Doses*, John Wiley & Sons, Inc., New York, 1986.

Weisbord, Marvin R., *Productive Workplaces, Organizing and Managing for Dignity, Meaning, and Community*, Jossey-Bass, San Francisco, 1991.

Weisbord, Marvin R., and 35 International Co-Authors, *Discovering Common Ground, How Future Search Conferences Bring People Together to Achieve Breakthrough Innovation, Empowerment, Shared Vision, and Collaborative Action*, Berrett-Koehler Publishers, San Francisco, 1992.

Chapter 10
Tool: Fishboning

The Memory Jogger, A Pocket Guide of Tools for Continuous Improvement, GOAL/QPC, 13 Branch Street, Methuen, MA 01844.

Sarazen, J. Stephen, "The Tools of Quality, Part II: Cause and Effect Diagrams," *Quality Progress*, July, 1990.

Chapter 11
Tool: Sticky Charting

Gitlow, Howard, S., Gitlow, Shelly J., Oppenheim, Alan, and Oppenheim, Rosa, "Telling the Quality Story," *Quality Progress*, September, 1990.

Chapter 12
Tool: Mindmaps to Mindscapes

Margulies, Nancy, *Mapping Inner Space*, Zephyr Press, 1991.

Margulies, Nancy, *Mapping Success*, video, 1993.

Margulies, Nancy, *Maps, Mindscapes and More*, video, 1993.

Wycoff, Joyce, *Mindmapping: Your Personal Guide to Exploring Creativity and Problem-Solving*, Berkley Publishing Group, New York, 1991.

Chapter 13
Tool: Storyboarding

Bunch, John, "The Storyboard Strategy," *Training & Development*, July, 1991.

DeMille, Richard, *Put Your Mother on the Ceiling*, Viking Penguin, New York, 1976.

Munn, Ph.D., Michael W., *Beyond the Borders, A Mythic Journey to Quality Consciousness*, unpublished manuscript, 1993.

"Storyboarding: Project Management II," *MindPlay*, Volume 4, Issue 2, Spring 1990.

Chapter 14
Tool: Computer-Aided Thinking

"Provoking a Brainstorm," *MacUser*, June, 1993

Ricks, Byron, "Luring Creativity," *Alaska Airlines Magazine*, June, 1992.

"Inspiration 4.0," *Macworld*, February, 1993.

DeGarmo, Scott, "Creative Attack!" *Success*, June, 1990.

INDEX

DATE DUE

DEC 1 2 2002	
MAY 1 5 2003	
FEB 1 4 2006	
APR 0 7 2009	

DEMCO, INC. 38-2931